ESSAYS ON THE WESTERN DECLINE

Norman D. Wallace-Swan
2024

TABLE OF CONTENTS

Introduction---4

Chapter One: Narrative Substructures---6

Chapter Two: Dharma and Adharma---10

Chapter Three: Adharmic Echoes---14

Chapter Four: Defending Hate---19

Chapter Five: Interregnum Tyrans---22

Chapter Six: Horseshoe Theory as Solipsism---28

Chapter Seven: Postmodern Manhood---31

Chapter Eight: The Nature of Power---34

Chapter Nine: Liberal Subversion---47

Chapter Ten: Literacy and Bureaucracy---51

Chapter Eleven: Meaning---57

Chapter Twelve: The Boomer Cruise---62

Chapter Thirteen: On Fortune---68

Chapter Fourteen: Regulation---72

Chapter Fifteen: Postmodern Traditionalism---80

Chapter Sixteen: Interregnum---98

Chapter Seventeen: Precipice---105

Chapter Eighteen: Reaction---113

Chapter Nineteen: Emergence---117

Chapter Twenty: Faith and Believing---122

Chapter Twenty-One: Cringe and Propaganda---128

INTRODUCTION:

The following series of essays stem from a number of years engaging in the ideas of Italian Elite Theory, cyclical history, and having to live within one of the most severely subverted nations in the world when it comes to Liberalism and Socialism: Canada.

Whether we are an experiment by power to test their ideological preconceptions on the nature of mankind, or we are an accidental conglomeration hellbent on self-destruction through the insane ramblings of true utopians, we still have the same problem. In this year of 2024, many still blame particular people like Justin Trudeau as exceptionally deranged for our problems. But I fear that is not the case, and that instead many Canadians have been instinctually subverted into a suicidal cult; some knowingly, others unknowingly. That the system moves as one, at least at every level of government, is concerning, and speaks to a deep rot within the power structure. That this is not merely at the upper levels, that it permeates the middle and base levels of all institutions, makes the issues we face, and its inevitable tragic ends, depressing in some ways.

However, even in the worst case scenario, where everything is subverted, every good person has turned bad, every weak mind is capitulated, there is still light at the end of the tunnel. This monstrosity is built upon a foundation of sand, held up by captives who fear the whip, or more so the coming end which they blind themselves to rather than face full force. For even within the subverted man, the serf man, the slave man, there lay within him an ever-present hope, an ever present faith. As you may see in the following essays, that faith is misplaced in the institutions, governments, and leadership.

What will come, perhaps if we cannot right this vessel soon enough, is great pain and suffering. Perhaps enough to make a believer of even them.

You will see many terms in this series of essays, such as *demoniac, narrative, coomer,* and I've done some work to make sure they are explained. If you have any questions, you can reach me on Twitter/X @LiquidSwan. Otherwise, thanks for purchasing my book, and enjoy this collection of essays.

CHAPTER ONE:

Narrative Substructures: Comparing Real and Fictional Perspectives

All conscious beings live in a narrative frame; they exist having knowledge of where they came from, where they are presently, and where they hope to be in the future. This is a journey of both time and space, a four dimensional journey.

Narratives come in many different forms, and follow familiar patterns. Not all narrative patterns are the same, though many share sets of ideas. Each individual plays the part of their own narrative protagonist (in as much as they are driven towards some goal, even if simply to exist). The protagonist has a particular viewpoint of the narrative frame, different from that of the perceived antagonist(s) within the same framework. Narratives tend to simplify the motivations of the people involved because human motivations can be complicated. We can logically deduce that in reality a protagonist is not merely a pure protagonist, as they possess elements within their character which inhibit their forward movement in the story. This is known as "auto-antagonism"; the sort of antagonism which occurs when people get in their own way which prevents their progress.

For example, not taking care of responsibilities, not taking care of grooming, neglecting duties to family, friends, employers or co-workers. These are things done that are counterproductive to purpose or goals. One could even surmise the self as the biggest antagonist one faces; and too, definitionally the largest antagonistic element we can hope to change (having direct control over it). It is easy to recognize if something is antagonistic: it gets in the way and prevents progress towards goals. One can recognize a particular narrative substructure through this understanding. The protagonist contains antagonistic elements. This creates a substructure in which the narrative antagonist is internalized. The idea being that if one wishes to "conquer" (or take care of) the world one must first conquer themselves. This internalization of the narrative antagonist is the bedrock of narrative individualism.

Another example of narrative substructure would be where the subject plays the part of the narrative protagonist. However in this narrative substructure he "externalizes" his narrative antagonist. He fails to conquer himself first and then attempts to conquer that which lies outside himself. There exist situations such as this where one must neglect their own antagonism and in complete and utter desperation flail in resistance to some overwhelming adversity, where there is no time for self-development, where one must fight for survival. But even after such a thing, after defeating whatever hydra or gorgon threatened them, they will remain frail and be consumed by their own pathological self-antagonism. It is a notion found in vast swathes of historical mythos, stories, legends. Like the war hero who becomes a drunkard consumed by vice and possessing little of virtue when the war is done and long over.

So let's explore the more common scenario. In this narrative frame the protagonist externalizes the antagonist, and uses whatever rhetoric or propaganda becomes necessary to explain his aims, goals, and ends. It creates a situation where the ends justify the means, by definition of the narrative frame being worked within by the protagonist. In the imagination, the protagonist of this narrative substructure of antagonist externalization may even come to defeat whatever foe he has spelled out before himself, but what is he to do now? He has vanquished his foe, and maybe the world hasn't changed to his expectations. There is something amiss! His ends have been met yet they do not reflect his imagination, his ideals. What is he to do? Should he turn inward and finally come to face his internal antagonism and progress himself onward towards self-improvement? Not likely. He is more likely to continue to play out the narrative in which he inhabits, because that is the narrative he has trained himself within. They must defeat some other external antagonist, the REAL and TRUE antagonist which he somehow missed earlier. But this time, he is looking for an excuse to make an antagonist of anything. He in effect invents and curates these antagonisms out of thin air. This destructive path leads to chaos and a reckoning which cannot be satiated except by equal oppositional force. When he begins to make the errors, creating antagonism where none exist, he creates victims, and in effect becomes a real antagonist towards others who are subject to his tyranny. As Nietzsche said, "Beware of fighting monsters, lest you become one."

So which narrative is fictional and which is true? Logically we must assume that reality, or the real world, presents us with non-fictional narrative frames. Real life is not a constructed narrative frame such as in Snow White, where clear narrative subjects are laid bare before you: Snow White is a protagonist, this is the ONLY possible viewpoint in the story, and the evil Queen is the narrative antagonist, and there is NO other possible viewpoint. If you were to change the viewpoints in such a story it would simply become a different story. This is because the story is a fiction, meant to convey a particular moral lesson (in the case of Snow White, one might take from it a lesson involving the dangers of vanity, amongst others). Narratives that are presenting moral lessons run only in one direction. The purpose of this is to make sure the lesson is clear, within its self-referential framing of the story. However, this peculiarity does not exist in real life, because real life comes from the viewpoints of several subjects, all purporting as the self-referential narrative protagonist. The problem arises when we start to reject that we are self-referential narrative antagonists. It is also important to note that we can act antagonistically towards other subjects, at least from their perspective. This might as well be the definition of empathy,

Rejection of the internalized antagonist in real life leads to projection of antagonism onto others, wherein the subject paints others as "bad" or "evil," and they then rationalize this projection post-hoc (after the fact). In the deepest sense of the term this behavior is a moral and ethical failure of the subject, because they fail to recognize and take responsibility for their own actions and behaviors and the negative impacts on others. This failure of self-examination can lead to extreme violence, because the subject has granted himself moral licence to act in such a manner, and so do with complete justification. In effect, the end-game of externalizing the narrative antagonist will, without exception, eventually bring the subject to become an actual antagonist which he is attempting to resolve, at least through the perspectives of subjects victimized by the person in question.

Internalized narrative antagonism leads to truth outcomes, whereas the substructures externalizing narrative antagonism lead to violence and suffering projected outwards. In conclusion, one can see this difference through thoughtful observation of the narrative perspectives of a given protagonist by how they view the outside world in relation to how they view themselves regarding antagonistic elements. This is certainly to greatly simplify this concept, though it may at first appear complicated.

CHAPTER TWO:

Dharma and Adharma: a Conflict of Fates

In time man must come to his senses and know when a wrong must be fixed. But how can man act to repair what is broken when so many forces undermine his propensity to act? Screeching degenerates? Cowards? Men without chests? FEAR THEM NOT! For there is only peril in the fear and they are nothing! They fear you! They fear us; this is why they screech slander at your good name, for they are the incapables, and you are their mortal enemy.

They hiss and squeal as you right your bow and rudder. But it is nothing more than the sound of lobsters dropped in a pot; you are become Chef, Bon Appetit.

Zombified hordes are not much to fear in the face of an organized elite. They are sheep without shepherds, wandering, while each one of them "knows" the way. It is naught but hubris, a malady of the mind driving them in all directions; chaos is their world, their weapon. What is ours?

You are the weapon. Your mind. Your ephemeral body. Your eternal soul. These are the same weapons our ancestors wielded in the face of their doom, and so here you stand today. Take one look at the enemy and know they are doomed. For those who hone these tools are to them proof of their weakness, their frailty, their spiritual squander.

You might cross Trans activists, LGBTQ+ idealists, and the like. They're propagandists. Everything they spout is a lie meant to force the rectangle of their delusion into the round hole of reality.

Their "evidence" lies in the face of biological fact. No more can you make a man into a woman, then can you turn a pineapple into a banana. You will find that they only accept "evidence" that directly supports their claim, and will reject anything which brings it into question.

But this is how these people are; do not take them seriously. Ask yourself this simple question when you come across them and their incessant crusade against anything and everything traditional: What would our ancestors say? Go back far enough and you would find they all agree that trans is a laughable joke that survives only now due to the low tides in which we find ourselves. Would it be tolerated at any other time? No, it would be silenced by whatever means necessary. No law needs writing, for it is a violation of the natural order.

Such is a symptom of our *interregnum tyran*, or what is often called "Democracy". Liberal though it may be called, it is merely liberal in the sense of senselessness. For what sense is there in suffrage? What value does it bring? It is a rearranging of the deck chairs on the Titanic, or worse, a feeble and ignorant submission to power.

We can pretend we only did what we were expected to do, yet we know this is a lie. Others are in a far worse position and actively think they are empowered, they believe in the mythology of the *interregnum tyran*. For those poor souls, they line up like bowling pins, standing like brave soldiers only to be knocked down each time. **Strike. Strike. Strike...** repeatedly, like a boot stomping on a human face, forever.

There is no salvation through interregnum, as such is the reservation of regnum, the platform upon which civilization and mankind flourishes and becomes unchained. Expansion into whatever new frontier becomes possible brings new possibilities for mankind. But for now, we remain chained by our weakness, our Kali Yuga nightmare of Liberty, Equality, and Fraternity. We are at liberty to drown in our sorrows, we are equal in our misery, and are an enfeebled fraternity bound by our chains and exile from prosperity.

The question becomes how do we bring about the regnum? Certainly one can imagine the end of such *interregna tyrannide*, but things could be worse. We could end up in an *anarcho tyrannide*. The *Demoniac (as mentioned in Chapter 16 of the Bhagavad* Gita, the ones firmly planted in solely materialism) always pulls. Death around every corner with no order whatsoever. Perhaps such is inevitable in the historical epoch and it too only needs to be overcome. Whatever the truth may be, it needs accounting for, in the great turning of the wheel. Crushing time (and thus people) like a great millstone, the Dharma turns gently and fertilizes upcoming cycles with the dripping of mankind's essence into the bowl upon which the Gods sup, *Ambrosia*. Fate surrounds us, masters us, puppeteering man and rearranging him whole. During the Kali Yuga, these forces act like gravity, driving civilization and its shepherd, mankind, into the depths, dashing the best of his flock upon the bedrock of hell.

But as iterated in Newton's Third Law: *"For every action (force) in nature there is an equal and opposite reaction."* Thus, the post-Kali Yuga rebound (the Dwapara) should be acceleratory. At some point, the dam which upholds the democratic tyranny will break, and what will come is the decision of valourous men. It can devolve into anarcho-tyranny, or the Golden Kingdom. For Tolkien, it would be the difference between Sauroman and Aragorn in his fictional epoch. It is the difference between Beowulf and Grendel. It comes down to the right man's will to righteous action.

Where do we find such a man? Can he be bred like the *Kwisatz Haderach* by the Bene Gesserit in Frank Herbert's *Dune*? Or battle-hardened like Julius Caesar and Alexander the Great? One thing is certain, the stage must be set for such a man to arise and take his place, and so to some degree, the future is truly out of our hands. But there is no reason to think something cannot be done, and as Krishna conveyed to Arjuna the importance of fighting adharma (adharma being the forces that attempt to run counter to dharma), Arjuna finally accepts his proper dharma in Chapter 18, Verse 73 of the Bhagavad Gita:

"**Arjuna said**: *O Infallible One, by Your grace my illusion has been dispelled, and I am situated in knowledge. I am now free from doubts, and I shall act according to Your instructions.*"

It is written in the dharmic cycle that the proper ordering of things is set in stone for ascension, but none are compelled. Ascension is only possible through blind faith, and many will stumble, fall, and fail. These treacherous contemplations, devour men like a whale does krill. Power, the One Ring, the Rubicon, the Siege of Vienna, the Fall of Constantinople, Stalingrad, the Alamo; in a word, **Sacrifice**.

CHAPTER THREE:

Adharmic Echoes: The Face of the Void

Creatures roam the interwebs like spiders at night, crawling across your pillow and seeking a warm place to rest. Nestling up to your head to absorb your dream-heat, while others jump into the snoring pit of doom, absent-mindedly, nightmarishly munched, but in dreamland, a crunchy, consciously forbidden snack.

People have opinions based on experiences, both their own and those of others. Many aren't great arbiters of reality, but we have little else. Thankfully these satisfy our need to function commensurate with survival. To deny your experience is to deny your being, so people cling to them like a man overboard to a life preserver. There is no worse suffering than ignorant blind suffering.

Some, having not experienced what you have, believe they are your better. Others simply go through life slipping on banana peels, repeatedly banging their heads on the floor, chalking it up to coincidence. Can such people be saved? Are they worth saving?

No. If someone has been so consumed by propaganda as to deny their pain and suffering, the avenues for redemption are limited. Pain is one of the most motivating things, and I do not mean just physical pain. Mental anguish is just as affecting if not more so than beatings. There are several Saadian (á la Gad Saad) idea pathogens which can lead to a state of insolubility of conscience, such as atheism, anarchism, and democratism.

Atheists surrender to materialism, and in doing so surrender faith. There is more to man than blood and bone, as bread alone does not fulfil his hunger. Anarchism presumes all men capable of self-rule, that such self-rule should or would result in order and organization, yet where are these great anarchisms? Furthermore, democratism is the idea that majority opinion and policy shall rule, and bring forth prosperity. This is like jumping from great height, and saying everything will stabilize when we hit terminal velocity. Such is true, but not useful or good.

So what makes these idea-pathogens rather than ideas? It is that they terminate into the Void. They lack a magnetic polar North to guide them objectively. In short, they lack the concept of God, a moral framework based outside of their material being. In claiming they hold the essence of being, and given they will one day perish, they embrace the Void. Such people are not promoting a thriving civilization, but are instead practicing adharma (in the Hindu/Buddhist sense), leaving them blind and malleable, holding no principles of function. Combine these with anarchy and majority rule, you have a recipe for chaos and disorder. This is why atheism is so dangerous: everything they do that is good derives from the remnants of their culturally imbued theism, whilst everything else is adharmic: unprincipled pleasure-seeking at any cost (for it is hardly theirs to bear). Heretics were not dealt with due to ignorance, but wisdom. It was maintenance; and control of decadence.

I will use the term adharmic to describe the atheist-anarchic-democratic going forward. By definition, adharmics cannot have or hold civilization. They are by nature, anti-civilizational; existing outside of time and negotiating only with themselves and their fellows. They cannot negotiate with the future or the past, because they "know" they will one day perish, and in the materialist view, that may as well be nothing. After them comes the all-consuming Void, the end, the great all-of-nothing, making their actions ultimately in their view, all-for-nothing. Holding a vision of the world which includes a transcendental overarching principle, means that the world existed before yourself, and will continue to exist long afterwards. You enter a contract that you will play your role accordingly, and so are held responsible for it. Ironically, the belief in the immaterial transcendental allows you to take possession of a part of it and do what you will with it. You are in that sense much more individualized and capable, productive and useful, than the adharmics. By what principle does an adharmic plant a tree under whose shade he will never seek shelter? From whose apples he shall never sup? One cannot point to the Void and claim that it drove him to it, for such reason lay beyond the Void.

Furthermore, what is a failure condition to the adharmic? For a Christian, Muslim, Jew, Jain or Sikh, failure is obvious; its consequences are known; atonement is prescribed. But for an adharmic? It is the Void if he does X; it is the Void if he does Y. It is the Void if he gives charitably; it is the Void if he murders. So what motivates him? How does he discern value or goodness? He who is not servant to the transcendental seeks to make the world serve him. The limiting principle? The Void. Tyranny is only restrained by their capacity. They may continue "common" religious virtues, but in as much as they do, they are not adharmic and so we cannot attest that to worship of the Void.

The unexhausted transcendental values which remain in an adherent of adharmism often trick such subjects into thinking they had them all along. Like the fish in water never knowing anything else, they have become blind to the medium in which they swim, and do not appreciate them until this medium is removed. In this, we demonstrate to the adharmic that theirs are not more than the worship of the self (and thus Void), and the only thing grounding them in the world of normalcy is that the "common" morals they cling to are not of them, but of civilization's transcendental principles. Many will claim they are consequentialists, but that is equally worship of the Void, only it restrains the actor to their transcendent principles to one layer of analysis. For example, they may claim that it is wrong to kill because they don't want to be killed (again, reference to the self). Which is literally to say: "I fear the Void, and so I assume you must fear the Void." However, that is hardly a principle, for when it comes to a question as to whom, of two (yourself and another) shall meet with the Void, how do you decide who shall do so? In the adharmic, it will be the self and preserve the self at any cost. There is no principle beyond the self and reference to the self regarding the Void.

Or how about if, considering consequentialism, you can go back in time to "kill baby Hitler"? Should you? Most adharmic consequentialists would say yes. However, did he think it through? If you kill baby Hitler perhaps Germany succeeds in getting the bomb first, perhaps the Final Solution plan succeeds instead of just doing a lot of damage. Perhaps instead of ~50 million souls being lost to war, 100 million or more are lost! So where is the value of consequentialism? You cannot foresee the consequences of your choices, and so assuming this prescience or at least your limited prescience on the issue is not a great method of deducing morality. It is less a moral system and more an abrogation of responsibility.

There are self-righteous, indignant adharmics everywhere, coming in all shapes, sizes, and ages. They are essentially radical egalitarians, who seek out "fairness". The world is not fair. The world is not equal. They don't care about our reality. If reality has a will they will bend it. They instead bend themselves, and you, to suit their narrative imposition. These faithless zealots will push their adharmic leisure, measure by measure, at their pleasure. They will take from you everything and do so with smugness. Their weakest versions call you an assortment of words ending in "-ist"; whilst their strongest order drone strikes to eliminate your family.

What can be done against such reckless disregard for reality and tradition? It depends on your place and time, but everyone can play a role. Some are better off being quiet soldiers, others should highlight the adharmics so others can see them glowing. If someone calls someone long dead or nearly an "-ist" word, challenge them, verbally accost them, but from the heart. Weak responses build upon other weaknesses, and we require strength, spiritual war requires boldness. The piles of bodies that can be counted from excess strength pales in comparison to that of weakness. Being strong and bold does not harm anyone but evil, and evil deserves it.

Men who genuflect towards the overbearing effeminate are not brave or strong, but cowards of the highest order. They are weak, and they know women do not want them naturally, that their only hope is to beg a woman to take them; in doing so they would pay any price no matter how deranged nor barren the womb. Fatherhood abates them. They fear responsibility. They are the men of excess, born to tear down the world our fathers and mothers built. They mock the old and wise. They favour the young and ignorant. They are the coomers, the entombers who seal our fate lest stopped. God saw fit that they are dealt with, for He made them cowards, and you dear reader are His bravest soldiers.

CHAPTER FOUR:

Defending Hate: A Manifesto Against Ugliness

There exist things worthy of disdain, and for every individual across time and space, hatred is a natural response. Why then, is there a prevailing narrative advocating for the abolition of hate? While the concepts of senseless, remorseless, and naïve hatred may be questionable, outright banning them raises intriguing questions about the temporality of hate.

This contemplation has lingered in my thoughts for many years. Hate, I argue, is an essential facet of human nature, serving as a mechanism for survival. This evolutionary adaptation shields us from both natural and social threats that could otherwise cause harm by: Identifying threats; enhanced vigilance; fosters in-group cohesion; imbues avoidance behaviours; and enforcement of positive social behaviours. It acts as a defence against pointless suffering, akin to love in its capacity to diminish human distress. The abolition of hate undermines humanity and the wisdom passed down through generations, rooted in real suffering that culminated in liberation from the Edenic Bestial Unconscious.

Would our current politically liberal elites, "enlightened secular humanist" leaders, (though some would identify as Marxists) guide us back to a bestial slumber, advocating for a return to Eden, a utopia of bliss and boundless abundance? The answer is a resounding no. Eden's gates are forever closed, and the loss of accumulated knowledge and experience awaits those who forsake the wisdom derived from God's grace in our liberation from the Edenic Bestial Unconscious.

These "leaders" advocate for "love" and "tolerance," and rightly so; however, extremes in either direction can be perilous. Excessive hatred can lead to unrelenting destruction, consuming the individual and perhaps erasing a part of the self forever. Similarly, an overpowering love can result in destructive consequences, from suffocating embraces to revealing vulnerabilities to adversaries. Temperance becomes our restraint, guiding us away from excesses, both material and emotional. Through the exercise of prudence, we strive to perceive the world beyond our superficial material and emotive states, finding beauty in a world saturated with sin and indulgence. Cautiously proceeding forward, we advance without faltering. To proceed without due caution will eventually bring our demise.

The proposition to abolish hate without addressing the excesses of love is untenable, and ugly, as both emotions, when taken to extremes, can be dangerous and corrupting. Recognizing the unworthiness of such a project, many rally under the ugly banners of love, riding out against hate. So, what will save the world, and how can one discern those seeking its destruction?

Drawing from my favourite author, Dostoyevsky, I posit: "Beauty will save the world." This quote appears in his novel "The Idiot." The context of the quote involves a discussion about the redemptive power of aesthetics, spirituality, and the transcendent in the face of the moral and existential challenges of the world. He was grappling with the idea that pure, selfless beauty has the potential to inspire and elevate the human spirit, leading individuals toward a higher moral and spiritual existence. In the novel, Prince Myshkin utters this phrase, and his character is often seen as a Christ-like figure, embodying qualities of compassion and innocence.

The quote suggests that the appreciation and pursuit of genuine beauty, whether in art, nature, or virtuous human actions, have the capacity to bring about positive transformation and salvation. It implies that the aesthetic experience, when grounded in truth and goodness, can serve as a powerful force for healing and redemption in a world fraught with moral complexities and existential challenges.

This is precisely what the true enemy, demoniac materialists, the people who care only for the pursuit of pleasure (at any and all costs), aim to annihilate — the suicidal destruction of beauty as an assault on existence itself. Identifying this, we must defend Beauty as the shining light upon the hill, not merely out of love for our kin or hatred for our rivals, but for the intrinsic value of Beauty itself. Beauty is worth defending, because ugliness is the alternative. It serves as a much more accurate compass than the virtues of anti-hate or even love.

Beauty is easy to detect. It is selfless sacrifice versus the selfish betrayal; it is the mother caring for their infant, in contrast to the murdering rapist; it is the father who goes out to work each day to provide for his family, in contrast to the abusive alcoholic father; it is the carved reliefs on the sides of buildings where it could have otherwise been left plain or blank; it is the offering of warmth to a suffering stranger versus the quiet dismissal or turning a blind eye to it; it is the gentle petting of a cat who crosses your path, versus treating the cat meanly.

Likewise, it is attending your father's funeral, versus ignoring the invitation; it is confessing your sins, versus taking them to the grave out of pride; it is the felt warmth from the sun on your face on the coldest winter day; it is to understand the innocent man upon the cross, and the guilt within each of us. All of these are forms within which a man partakes in his life, and there are many more. But that a man might take them, might live them, might be them, might suffer them: that is the beauty of being which saves the world against darkness. We hate, because we love, in the name of beauty.

CHAPTER FIVE:

Man, Woman, and the Interregnum Tyrans:
Balancing, not battling, the Sexes

In what I call the postmodern interregnum tyrans, there is an ever expanding and unhealthy conflict between the sexes. This gulf must be closed and if it is unnaturally prevented from doing so it will bring continuous disaster. Men and women need each other in proper balance, to regulate their essential being, both physically and spiritually. What is it which divides us from each other? What must be done or undone?

In physics there is a force that attracts atoms to each other based on the prevalence of electrons on a particular side of the atom, which, though negatively charged, weakly attract a place of electron prevalence to a side of electron infrequency. This however only becomes noticeable in absence of other more significant forces which might cause different orientations and balances. Such is a metaphor for postmodern men and women.

Liberalism imagines that a freeing individualism and individuation must result in betterment for the individuals involved. This may even be true, but there is more to a person than that person themselves. An individual is a conduit of culture, society, and power. Through them, aligned with others, is the structure in which society rests, deploys itself, and dare I say, expires. There is an instinct of civilization, whether tribal or of higher complexity, to reassert itself and re-create itself in various iterations in order for the civilization to proceed. However, in our case I am speaking of organic civilizations.

There could very well exist inorganic civilizations,

but none which are guarded, tamed, and built by organic beings. Organic beings like ourselves will always give ourselves precedence over the inorganic, even if we do so kicking and screaming. Likewise, while many of our human family march towards the great "ruining" bottleneck of antinatalism, is it not but a base-level rejection of the current state of things? There are of course some happy couples who choose not to have children, but there are too those who will never couple. This is in essence, masturbation. Couples or individuals who purposefully do not procreate nor seek out a partner for procreation, are not maintaining their legacy. When they have intercourse it is masturbatory, and a waiver from their duty as living, breathing beings. Masturbation is all an inorganic civilization could achieve, and for this reason one could compare antinatalism as inorganic.

As man becomes ever more isolated from woman, his internalized femininity (InFem) must sprout outwards to compensate, for if not he would perish. Likewise as a woman becomes ever more isolated from man, her internalized masculinity (InMasc) must sprout outwards or she too would perish. These opposing internal essences, which are difficult to spell out, become aged, poorly seasoned; becoming rancid and marking sufferers with a distinctive energy. Normal people will avoid them (and should!) which reduces their dating pool to the dregs. This is the result of a lack of other forces, leading to the weak effect of attraction of the internalized aspects of masculine and feminine conjoining in the individual. Such a person is either instinctually subverted or broken beyond regular repair.

But why would they perish? As men or women are isolated they age in abnormal ways. There is no push or pull, only the ceaseless drudgery of being alone or pining over the past. This might breed entitlement or envy, and so their development arrests. This further isolates the individual from their instincts, leading to resentment. Some cope through retreating to fantasy, whether gaming, masturbation, or masturbatory practices like having unproductive intercourse with a temporary or otherwise instinctually subverted partner. They will often get to periods of self harm going as far as suicide attempts or even a completed tragedy. Death in their 50s and 60s is common, leaving the corporeal realm more than a decade sooner than their peers. It is a dark subject, a stark future, perhaps best exemplified by the opening paragraph of the unnamed narrator main character in Dostoyevsky's "Notes from the Underground":

"I am a sick man.... I am a spiteful man. I am an unattractive man. I believe my liver is diseased. However, I know nothing at all about my disease, and do not know for certain what ails me. I don't consult a doctor for it, and never have, though I have a respect for medicine and doctors. Besides, I am extremely superstitious, sufficiently so to respect medicine, anyway (I am well-educated enough not to be superstitious, but I am superstitious). No, I refuse to consult a doctor from spite. That you probably will not understand. Well, I understand it, though. Of course, I can't explain who it is precisely that I am mortifying in this case by my spite: I am perfectly well aware that I cannot "pay out" the doctors by not consulting them; I know better than anyone that by all this I am only injuring myself and no one else. But still, if I don't consult a doctor it is from spite. My liver is bad, well—let it get worse!"

All our life plays out as a narrative of being. It is perhaps impossible for humans to live otherwise and it is likely we cannot perceive reality itself outside of this framing. Man living without woman and vice versa, is to live a narrative of solipsism. Together, the narrative characters contain the spirits of countless ancestors they could never have known, and the experiences they've had with those they have. These ancestral spirits arise as our unsubverted instincts, playing out in an (ideally) natural narrative drama in which we "act our role" with our partner. This partnership narrative should be an escape from the societal propaganda which continuously surrounds us, allowing for a sense of normalcy despite the chaos and subversion. In these "gardens" of narrative, we should find fruitful abundance, and thus springs natalism, the rebirth of the struggle for being, in the form of procreation and the raising of healthy children.

The narrative partnership is like a battle, with two people building a stronger and stronger bond through real shared suffering and struggle. If they are victorious they will build a relative empire; if they fail then it will be despite their strength or because of their weakness. But how is an individual, with little experience, to know who would make a good partner for them in their narrative? Does a character know who will be best to venture forth with? No, such is done and organized by authors who compose a narrative arc, wherein the actors play their part. Should we author our own narrative? Perhaps some are capable, but many more are not. Who shall pair these types? Who shall organize these people into productive and meaningful stories?

This is where tradition is invaluable. Older people who have acted in their narrative relationship, who have experienced the uniqueness of such a thing, should organize the young into fruitful partnerships. Parents, Grandparents, Uncles, Aunts, and Godparents, should do such work to help people figure this out. Not without the consent of the people involved of course, assuming they are not subverted. We cannot truly train people for these plays, these roles. They must be learned and experienced. But with the proper attitude, it is possible. The process is natural. It should not be forced, unless there is subversion in which case they can make arrangements to deal with that first. But some people are not worthy of pairing with someone else because they are broken, and this will rob the other party of a potentially happy life. There are stragglers in every herd. Nature is brutal.

As the parties to a relationship struggle together, they damage each other. This must happen and inevitably will (to some extent, varying in each particular narrative). This constant destruction and rebuilding keeps the male *InFem*, and the feminine *InMasc* in check, keeping the wife feminine and the husband masculine, as balance requires for stability. Without this natural balance, the individual becomes an amorphous greying blob in maintainence mode, for the growth has been retarded and then halted.

Subversion

Subversion comes in many forms. Some subversion is systemic: mass consumable food laced with hormones, plastics, and drugs. Birth control for example is a sort of brainwashing for women, for it alters their hormones which alters their perspectives on reality and thus the narrative frame of their relationships. Chemicals in our water and food supplies likely have some sort of effect on our endocrine systems as well, and we can see through obesity rates, things have drastically changed in our population. Food is also simply less healthy than it used to be.

What does this do to children? If you have been subverted, then they are being raised in an environment that to them is totally normalized and thus, adapting to this requires subversion. Children are quite disregulated in these situations. In a divorce situation, though not ideal, children can turn out fine if both parents work to be regular. Divorce stems from poor mate selection, and should be largely preventable, but even if reinstated, it is better to be from a broken house than to be raised in one.

Cultural subversion attacks normal sex relations by interfering directly with mating narrative formation. By establishing one (normally the female) as a victim. This disables the female normative relations with the male, which allows the creeping of InFem and InMasc into the dynamics as the feminine position goes unchallenged. This also brings more of the male InFem to sprout and grow, leading to an overly lunar scenario of perpetual darkness. The same but opposite effect is in the female and the subverted wife will become more masculine. This creates a spiral which destroys the family unit, and if this happens for a long time, civilization itself. The solution is to embrace the instinct, regulated by custom and tradition.

The subversion of our instincts becomes a twisted simulacra, a warped and unnatural compromise to postmodernity and Liberalism. It is a spiritual murder-suicide, for an individual alone cannot contend with the world via spiritual solipsism. He or she must always be in a productive conflict, or our InFem/InMasc will annihilate us, leaving us a neutered, grey, and sex-neutral soul, devoid of personality, happiness, fulfilment, generosity, kindness, or love. Subversion means we no longer act, but are acted upon as passive objects and yet some claim that gives us objectivity, but nothing could be further from the truth.

CHAPTER SIX:

Horseshoe Theory as Solipsism: Liberalism is only One Point of View

Horseshoe theory, proposing similarities between the extremes of left and right, has often been viewed as simplistic. While any concept can be framed to fit a particular narrative, the idea of Liberal-Centrism, where liberals position themselves as centrists, distorts reality. According to this perspective, all other ideas merely orbit the liberal truth, lacking the harmony of Liberalism.

However, such solipsism ignores real grievances highlighted by both left and right, a phenomenon observable from various perspectives. Conservatives, for instance, may similarly argue against Liberalism and Marxism, positioning both as planets orbiting the greater conservative truth, exposing the arbitrary nature of this theory. The "centre" in each case projects its "horseshoe" outward onto the world, revealing the inner workings of the mind more than objective reality.

This projection of claims indicates narrative dominance, and succumbing to the view of power as oppositional results in domination. Rejecting this madness projection, a sensible centrist (traditionalist) can center their worldview through objective and spiritual anchors lacking in their rivals. Traditional views, often dismissed as "expired," have endured since the dawn of humanity, surviving through constant trial and error. In contrast, other ideas may require volumes of suffering to achieve the same understanding. Historical examples, such as the Levée en Masse during the French Revolution, highlight the consequences of forsaking traditional values for ideological fervor.

As we stand in 2023, less than 235 years since the Estates General in 1789, leadership is in disarray, the economy precariously balanced, and societal malaise growing. The acid of Liberalism corrodes our resolve, turning humanity into a formless mass, centralizing systems with contempt for dissent. Inaction is the true fear, as delay only intensifies suffering. The enemy, ideologically driven, rejects debate and discussion, opting to destroy rather than admit faults. They force degeneracy on the young, labelling dissenters intolerant, racist, or [Insert-term-here]-phobic, while disrespecting native religions and promoting external ideologies.

The looming issue of Medical Assistance in Dying (MAiD) in Canada, initially intended for end-of-life situations, has expanded irrationally. By Spring 2024, the mentally ill, homeless, and impoverished will have the option of MAiD, adding to the societal erosion where bonds are frayed and meaning is scarce. Competent leadership, absent from committee decisions, is necessary to confront this degenerate malaise. Mercy in this regard is entropic weakness; doing the right thing, though unpopular, is essential. The call for democracy's dismissal arises from the belief that normies lack the foresight for long-term good. Steering the Ship of State requires a competent captain, not a committee. The alternative is a Great Man, a singular vision that can navigate the complexities of governance and society.

This Great Man, Caesar, embodies the true will of the people, directing and shepherding their lives, reforming order into the human form. This figure stands against the forces of entropy and degeneracy, rejecting the feminized committee and the chaos of democracy. In each productive act, the Great Man lives, sculpting and painting the nation into a true aesthetic form, bringing life and vitality without diminishment. The alternative is continued suffering without meaning or purpose.

Yet one might question the idea of an autocrat, and while it is indeed questionable, there is no question regarding our current trajectory: decline; and so my point is not to propose a perfect solution, but merely a solution to our current malaise. Who knows what will trudge forth after that, all we know is at the current rate, ever down we go.

CHAPTER SEVEN:

Postmodern Manhood: Reduction

While thinking back into the past, we reach spiritually into the immaterial realm. None of what was remains in the present besides what we remember. In a sense, this differentiates man as a creature from most other animals. The addition of this aspect of man in itself is one of the key characteristics which allows man to transcend the material world, the world of strain and suffering, to become invigorated in spirit, to self-actualize and expand themselves apart from their material struggles. Why seek this out? Relief. What does this mean? Redemption. Men are usually content with their material worries, and hardly think beyond their day-to-day. They never experience a spiritual moment throughout their lives despite knowing they will one day, die.

They will be in a state of shocked confusion bearing witness to those who pass-on around them, whom they knew well, those will be painful, short-lived reminders of mortality. Are they reminded of their bounded time? I do not know, but I imagine the majority don't consider this. This is discarded, tossed like trash. Such doesn't leave the issue alone, in their minds. Each instance of "being" is met anew by emotions, each step forward is another short chapter in the unfolding limited existence. One day, they will no longer *be*.

This is fear. Awful fear. All men feel it. It's part of living. This abyss is irrefutable, undeniable. Religion used to hold the hands of men, guiding them through this struggle and giving them hope and purpose. Most struggle to navigate this terrain alone.

Perhaps what is needed is for men to seek moral guidance, endowed with spirit, a will, something larger than themselves or purpose. Perhaps Mediaeval spiritualism is lost forever. There ought be something there, something to hoist oneself up higher to avoid deep pits of narcissism and indulgence. If God is dead (as Nietzsche said), our duty as men becomes the rescue of the Heavenly Father, Son, and Holy Spirit within the depths of our souls.

Atheists no doubt find this troubling, and it's hard to blame them; they were not raised in it, they weren't ready for it. No child should reach adulthood without spiritual endowment, even some basic ancient wisdom. In the end it matters not whether one believes God to be the Supreme Being ruling all life from his seat in Heaven, or instead, is the psychological embodiment of thousands of years of ancient wisdom. In the Postmodern era it's all the same. The Postmodern man is, without the spiritual, adrift upon the sea, doomed, so to speak, to kick and paddle pathetically with his legs dipped in the waters in a vain attempt to get...anywhere. Desperation exposes us to the oceanic depths.

Wind blows over man as he kicks. Does he have the sail but know not how to use it? It's an equal failing as much as not having one, and so we see that despite a material possibility he isn't availed until the immaterial sail enters his mind. The situation is hopeful, but precarious until he overcomes the limit of material thinking. It's wrong to assume this analogy proposes a land to which this sailing man could rest himself. No such a place exists. No land, only endless sea. To plant man's civilization upon land turns it to stone, to make it dead. Man's civilization is moving, living, breathing, and dies out when its heart stops. Before it dies it must pass on its heartbeat.

We can hope to help others learn to sail, be they willing students. Some can't be helped for they will not take it upon themselves. We can endow our descendants with knowledge, taking from ancient wisdoms, keeping them alive as our own hearts pass into stillness.

This light of civilization is a delicate flame venturing across an endless sea, held by man alone, passed through enormous effort to the next generations, each time being even more miraculous than the last. Many don't understand the vision required for this. It's certainly divine intervention. Whether you believe this intervener is "God", or a reliable and time-tested guide, the material world shows us what the world and reality appear to be, but it's the immaterial which guides man how to go one's way in it; without it, our light goes out and we are cast upon the sea to perish.

Behold, Man! May his sails hold tightly to the wind, divined through the breath of life endowed by his creator, whatsoever that might be.

CHAPTER EIGHT:

The Transformative Nature of Power: Power Transforms the Radical and Idealism Dies

The gates breach.

Old structures crumble; old ways are cast away. The radical explained their plan. A wrecking ball swung towards us, our eyes cast upon its force and we gasped in horror at the terror. Suddenly, the destruction halts. Why?

Their nature changed. People seek to steer power, but power itself guides the wheel. This is history. Power rarely shifts and even rarer it is for such a shift to persist. "Revolutions" are fueled by a romantic passion, like a love story sweeps people away to pursue transcendency. Transformation and revolution is rarely logical, rational, or executed as it is felt.

-The Rollercoaster-

Power carries a feeling of inflated romance. One imagines the things one will do with this new "love"; an unbelievable romance, a rollercoaster to the heights of positive emotion, but one cannot see the direction. At the peak, is the precipice of positive feelings. Relief. Suddenly, the coordination is off. Romance disappears. The ground rushes up. One holds onto the faintest hope until the end. Reality rushes in, flooding expectations to the abyss. It's the transformation of power.

-The Elephant and His Rider-

Power is a minority ruling over a majority. The minority is in precarity, but they benefit from being sovereign. It's indifferent whether the political system is democratic or dictatorial as each is minority rule. It is possible for the majority to be free under a monarchy, while shackled under a democracy. The majority is an elephant; the minority is its driver. The driver must be cautious controlling the elephant, as control is fickle, ultimately at the mercy of the elephant's emotions. Historically, the driver is thrown and stomped into oblivion. The driver's reason and logic matters not to the elephant, as it is irrational, fickle, erratic, and impulsive. It's permanently this way. This is the *mob*. This is taken from the comparison of human psychology made by social psychologist Johnathan Haidt of New York University.

Just as the mob will cast off its leaders, new leaders arise from the chaos to again take the reins. People ask,

"What would you do with power?"

This is the question for our representatives when we ask them,

"What is your political platform?"

-And then what?-

An election is held; voters are disappointed in the results. They were told the plan and voted. It was reasonable, but failed to manifest. Why? The elephant gets a new driver after crushing the previous, and it's no different than before. The mark of a good driver is skilled negotiation with the overwhelming destructive enormity while getting provision and sustenance, while steering this leviathan in a way which benefits all. The driver makes promises of all sorts and the elephant allows him limited credit. But if his emotions are so-toyed, destruction becomes its will and the elephant always collects.

Another will replace the previous, and the cycle will continue. Prospective drivers gaze up, and see the current driver corralling it, ignorantly thinking the driver's height makes it easy. Why such a fuss about driving it; why do these drivers fail? People overestimate their own capacity. They realize how difficult a job it is only once they are in it. Captaining ships looks pretty simple to the uninitiated, but operating a ship is complex, taking years of training and decades of combined crew experience. Ask many though, and they will tell you exactly how it's done because they saw a film once.

-The Thin Line which Veils-

Analogies are useful visualizations, but we need to apply it and address framing. Do politicians steer the nation, or the opposite? It would not be proper to say one or the other but it is also not equal. Political science is the attempt to define the divide.

This divide is hubris and humility, the avoidance of catastrophe. Politicians invent problems, and convince people of solutions. If people are unimpressed with the plans, they won't allow him power, and will elect or submit to someone capable. One of the problems of democracy is its basis in the irrational mob. Measuring human progress by wealth or infrastructure, democracy is not causal. It isn't infrastructure development itself, but the liberty to act. It is important to emphasize that progress is determined by infrastructure development, done best with (internally) open and free markets.

-Logic, Liberty, and Law: Form and Wealth-

Logic shows that free markets rapidly build infrastructure. Evidence demonstrates this. It has little to do with democracy, but instead economic liberty. The top nation in the world for GDP per capita (in 2020) is Qatar. Qatar is a Monarchy, it's Head of State an Emir, not a president. Of the top ten GDP nations, five are a form of dictatorship or monarchy (Qatar [1], Singapore [3], Brunei [5], United Arab Emirates [7], Kuwait [8]), four are small, highly developed European representative democracies (Luxembourg [2], Ireland [4], Norway [6], Switzerland [9], and the United States ranks tenth. Chinese free market zones, Macau [2] and Hong Kong [11], would be ranked very closely in this group if they were counted on their own (outside of China). This wealth is the result of a free market system, which allows for the free flow of goods and services. Of the lowest ten GDPs per capita, you have a series of socialist states, democratically elected governments which take the shape of a corrupt dictatorship, and unstable regimes. Venezuela [unranked] and Syria [unranked] are too corrupt and chaotic to be measured; Burundi [185] an impoverished presidential republic; Central African Republic [184] an incredibly poor presidential republic; The Democratic Republic of the Congo [183] a democratic state again, poor; followed by Eritrea [182]; Niger [181]; Malawi [180]; Mozambique [179]; and Liberia [178]; all making under 1500 "International dollars" average GDP per year. All of these are democracies (or Socialist states) which cannot get it together enough to escape poverty.

Some would criticize these points by saying they were corrupt democracies or were not "truly" socialist states. Those are not very good criticisms. Firstly, if democracy were causal for wealth, why are they still poor? If it isn't causal for corruption, why are they so corrupt? There is no proof that democracy is what foments wealth, but liberty of action. Detractors don't consider the individual but instead look at the collective will, and view things from the end rather than the beginning, putting the cart before the horse.

-Judging Cause from Ends: a Dangerous Miscalculation-

Observe the economy. You consume shoes, the detractor will say that you couldn't have bought those shoes had the seller not procured them. But the seller couldn't have procured those shoes for sale without a supplier. That supplier in turn couldn't have supplied those shoes without a manufacturer. The manufacturer couldn't have made those shoes without material suppliers, and in turn those suppliers couldn't have those supplies without the raw materials, and those materials require some form of harvesting. So you see, the detractor says, it took the collective will to produce those shoes, these shoes cannot possibly have been manufactured without collective action. They conclude collectivism produces things, and individuals cannot.

The detractor is wrong. It wasn't collectivism making those shoes. No central planning created them. None of the people in the supply chain were friends. Each part of it consisted of self-interested individual actions. These individuals cooperated to produce and sell shoes, but at no point did any *collective action* take place. Individualism doesn't entail one single person does all, but that each person acts in their own interest. No one in cooperative production acted to produce shoes, they only acted in order to extract value from their particular actions.

The leather-maker for the shoe manufacturer perhaps also supplies for the manufacture of belts, jackets, and ...pants. Everywhere touched by central planning is less productive than places LACKING this. High productivity in a planned economy happens DESPITE central planning, universally. Outliers are comparisons of imperfect scenarios in every case (less free versus more free). In a perfect world the cause and effect would be clear. However, we have foggy and muddied vision and are stuck with relativity. The logic supports free markets: where people are more free to act, unbound by bureaucracy and paperwork, the faster infrastructure will develop; wealth increases, with people growing richer. The inverse is also true.

-Death by a Thousand Good Intentions-

The world is imperfect, fallen. People rule emotionally. The problem isn't a lack of leadership, hidden intentions, laziness, or irreverence. Power transforms people. Power gives insight into the previously unknown. Power blinds, rushing a weak leader's head into the clouds, separating him from reality. Solutions cannot come from politicians who only act, but who enhance individual liberty of action. Only through this can things improve, the negotiation amongst individuals cooperating for mutual benefit, and the benefit of all. Regulation and statutes cannot build infrastructure. By-laws, building codes, victimless crimes, are irrecoverable damages.

Following the logic of regulators, roots it in the same

arguments which support feudal serfdom. Calls for "order" appear reasonable, because the counter-position is "chaos". Let's examine this "logic". Regulators argue that we must control the public-facing aspects of people's lives, because they could interfere with the wellbeing of others. This has led to regulations on building, employment, and business (among others). Building regulations act as a set of state-enforced restrictions limiting individual action concerning building projects.

The concept starts well-intentioned (public safety) but ultimately fails. Housing is a market, a system of supply and demand. Regulations create an entry barrier. With any barrier, entry is limited; creating a ceiling that excludes many, legally halting some from doing the "non-ideal", despite being an improvement for them. Otherwise if some wanted they could take their land and develop it in a way that doesn't negatively impact others so that it is more useful, on the lower-end market, creating a low bar for entry. These need not be unsafe nor dangerous, simply inclusive. Regulations make this a legal impossibility; the State through its by-laws brings "order" with force, destroying these buildings which don't meet the "regulatory standards", despite being safe and used by parties of their own free choice. In such a case the "meeting" of 'standards' is submission to them.

Many defend this, feeling order is foundational. But people are priced out, they become homeless or reliant upon charity or welfare, becoming demoralized. These people become economic deadweight as they aren't self-reliant; in this setup there is incentive to stagnate instead of risking overcoming it. The incentives are the problem.

This raises all bars, decreasing competition, while increasing costs. Any regulation must be enforced (at cost). The more influential you are the less it will affect you, but it isn't free. Where many could be housed in low-cost shelter, they now must live in full-cost, fully wired, fully plumbed, and fully regulated homes. The result ideally would be that everyone gets to have a fully regulated home. This is the ideal that the supporters claim to aim at, but have never and will never achieve. Instead there is shortage; people resort to living in camper vans, tents, couch surfing, cars, dumpsters, alleyways, doorways, or storage units. We live in a fallen world, and these regulations come from shortsighted idealists sitting in ivory towers proclaiming their superiority to the plebeians, which takes the form of the managerial conquest we see today.

-Red Tape: Directing The Masses to Serfdom-

Arguments for regulation come from existing homeowners, who exercise their influence to disrupt the market needs of those who don't hold property. By exercising political power to manipulate the market through regulations in their political sphere, they guarantee that their own property will rise in value by leveraging state force to inflate their property values.

I ask, how is this not considered corruption? It is public theft to apply public resources in order to benefit a party maintaining the power held by that party in the market. This isn't unique to housing, nor is it to our socio-political paradigm. It spawns from utopianism. Many autocrats believe utopia is possible: that by their design alone they can manipulate the world and mankind into perfection. Do they not know why our ancestors termed it Utopia, which literally means "no place", as in "impossible to exist place"?

Power held by feeble-minds is more dangerous than giving a loaded handgun to a toddler; they don't understand the violent potential of the weapon, nor the consequences of its use. They cannot control it. Outside of experience, there's no determining who's weak-minded. Autocratic thinking is not itself indicative. An autocrat somewhat understands power. The real indication of a weak mind is one which proposes and believes in Utopia. They believe their idea is unique (naïveté). It's difficult to reason with them, for how does one convince them that their Utopia ("no place") is simply barbarism? They don't think it through.

They reframe evidence like with the: "real communism was never tried", a "no true Scotsman" logical fallacy. Since "true" communism requires a Utopia, anything that doesn't or hasn't achieved Utopia must not be communism; what they are really saying is that communism is logically impossible. Weak-minded people exist throughout the world. Utopians ignore suffering, and are unsympathetic sociopaths more concerned with their vision than of the suffering masses.

Suffering is reality. It's a privilege to overcome the natural state of being: complete and utter impoverishment, the state of shivering cold, near starvation, zero allies or friends, being constant prey, despotic hopelessness punctuated by a self-realisation of worthlessness. That's mankind, and it's overcome by taming the world, harnessing it, making it work for man, rather than laying down and being ever victim to it.

-The Nature of Power is a Natural Law-

Power is deep, resounding from the origins of man. Humble leaders lead societies more successful than those with hubristic leadership which ignored the world around them for their own vision of how things ought to be. But an *ought* doesn't make for an *is*. Over aeons, this competence was tested, leading to selected standards that remain true today. First you cannot ignore the suffering of your people (beware of liars.) Second, you cannot substitute for reality and must always be aware of your capacity to be blinded by ideals: none are immune to propaganda. Third, don't mistake your position in power for invulnerability: you are but flesh and bone and as interchangeable as any flesh and bone; you must be a cognizant mind, and hone your perception. Fourth, it isn't just thinking nor perception, but acting and doing, which leads.

Failure is death. Any challenge to you, you must be martial. The sword is mightier than the pen. The might of the pen is a bastardization of reality, it's a coping mechanism for the weak. It's only true symbolically in time as the pen directs the narrative villainizing the sword, but in the present the sword is always victorious. Be a sharp sword, especially amongst swords, and you will be better for it. The pens will write. You live and exist in material reality, while infamy is immaterial. The only rational purpose for power outside of personal wealth and infamy is to advance human wellbeing, through the expansion of societal infrastructure in order to reduce the state of poverty which mankind is naturally in. That's how it's classically perceived, those leaders who have ushered in great works, and great technologies, are remembered as pioneering heros; while destroyers are remembered as villains. The sword decides.

-The Power of the One Ring-

The Radical's self-perception is of revolutionary uniqueness. They are wrong. There has always been competition. The framing isn't that the radical sees themselves as a power-centre in competition with existing nodes, for they compete to be power-wielder. The power-centre remains unchanged. It is more stoic, cold, strong, and resilient than generations of radicals. When the radical moves into power they can't radicalise it. They're only capable of wielding it or tyrannising it. In wielding it they're possessed by it, unified within it, overwhelmed by it. If alternatively they tyrannize it, they won't be able to overcome weakness, becoming consumed in their effort to wrestle control from the narrative substructures of that society. All will recognize the tyranny, and then it's only a matter of time before collapse. Tyranny is temporary, as is radical power. The narrative substructures overpower them, making the surviving radical cohort conservative.

Over time the power structure tames radicals, their aims unachieved. There are examples: Chancellor Angela Merkel of Germany; former President of Brazil Dilma Rousseff; former US President Barack Obama, all radical in their beginning, and now consumed by the machinery of state. It isn't coincidental that leaders of different nations went through this phenomenon. It isn't age, Obama promised radical change during his first campaign for President, like universal healthcare within his first term. Failure; his radicalism tamed, not by age but by the power structure.

The same for President Rousseff. Raised in an upper-class conservative family with an immigrant father, she attended conservative schools until his death in 1962. In 1964 she began attending public school, and was taught by socialist teachers, which (in short) lead her to become a socialist revolutionary. On the discussion of violent or gradual change, she sided with violent means after reading French intellectual Régis Debray. Unbeknownst to her conservative family, her group COLINA robbed banks, killed police, stole cars and did two bombings (no casualties in that case). She was later captured, jailed, and tortured with beatings and electric shocks by the Brazilian Military Junta. Decades later, we find her in a political career dogged by corruption paralleled only by the worst years of authoritarian rule. Long did she stare into the abyss it would seem. It stared back and impregnated her with the Brazilian disease of official malfeasance. She promised radical reforms, but what happened? Nothing. She was impeached in her second term and is now powerless.

The Shrew was tamed. "O megara foi domada."

Patterns like this persist in all systems because power structures conserve, otherwise they would dissolve, so change only happens when the structure's narrative consents.

-Dropping the Plunger-

The radical sees power structures that they are a part. It isn't logical that every person bears an equal burden of complicity within this structure, but all bear some. This is the origin of the social justice claim about the structure problem and that it must be torn down and begun anew. To tear it down would be disastrous and accomplish none of the ideals they purport. The "year zero" they aim for never works. You cannot root out past suffering and bring justice, just injustice. There's no satisfaction in resentment, only suffering. To destroy the structure would maximize the necessity of conserving whatever remains, leading to ultra-conservatism.

Evidence of history, mythology, and religion proves this. It's proven through logic. As stated earlier, infrastructure takes work and time. This has value if we value prosperity. Any destruction of infrastructure increases suffering. If the desire to increase suffering is evil then destroying infrastructure is evil. Therefore wishing destruction is evil. The sensible must abandon Marxism, or they are evil.

Leftist idealism is perverse. Individuals are victims if they aren't equal, believing collectivism will restore Eden. This isn't true. Actions are individual. Even an embrace with a beloved, is two individuals. Leftists promote collectivism, unconscious to the collective social effort from which all prosper.

"Equality," economic flattening, is based on individual resentment and greed. It is a false god. "Eating the rich" is a farmer eating his seed grain. You may be hungry in the midst of winter, doomed. That seed grain sits there tempting you. Eating it may satisfy you for a time, but will crush you into dust. You have doomed your future self to oblivion. But if you instead suffer, you may get to live, and maybe in prosperity. People don't look at the property of others and think that it's the result of the collective effort of millions, but it is! The leftist sees only greed and malice in people. They cannot see past this. They don't realize that wealth doesn't have anywhere else to go, that wealth is an abstraction of productivity, and a feedback system to reward progress and efficiency, while punishing damages or inefficiencies.

People don't get wealthy for damaging infrastructure and harming society's development, they get wealth for both the maintenance of and expansion of infrastructure. The wealth earned is society holding them to account and rewarding their contributions. Everyone contributing gets rewarded, some a little more and some a little less.

-Resentment of Being makes for Hell on Earth-

The scales vary but are structurally universal. There isn't an alternative to this framing. It's an accurate assessment of how things work. I reject that resentment is meritorious, instead of anti-human, and anti-individualist. Marxism and social justice is anti-cooperative. They don't see the voluntary, cooperative collectivism capitalists et al find themselves in, and want to replace it with involuntary collectivism. That's the historical result. They point to individuals who aren't as successful as others, left behind by technological advancement, tragedy of being, or any grievance imaginable. Should they be cared for? Should they be abandoned? Well, all life is as the Red Queen states in "Through the looking Glass":

"Now, here, you see, it takes all the running you can do, to keep in the same place. If you want to get somewhere else, you must run at least twice as fast as that!"

Some are left behind, but we're human beings, not machines. We engage in charitable works, to lift others up. It isn't a requirement, but an act of good, an act of goodwill if you goodly will. This is faith, that those helped will help themselves and be raised from suffering. What's the alternative? Entitlement; not just laze and sloth, but to the fruits of others. There is no case for this entitlement, it's a farce. It's an act of injustice. If you want a part you must be a party to it. The alternative is parasitism. Suffering despite society is a choice. Suffering is the return to your natural state, and the self is to blame.

There are real victims of crime. I don't mean to remove justice, but enhance it. If someone harms you then you should be made whole. Within a society there are more heroes than villains, but when you dispossess heroes from their works by giving it to the state, you lose the heroes and keep the villains. State welfare disempowers individuals. It dispossesses them of their chance to contribute, and forces them into weakness, sterility, entitlement, and disillusion. They persist as postmodern serfs: labouring grievances instead of land.

The Marxian notion of collectivism is flawed. It chastises capitalism for not tending to failed individuals, and it demands the voluntary and peaceful collective action taken within the free market (uncoerced) must be cancelled in favour of coercive force because of "inequality". However it is different: a resentful chaos-producing, utopian ideal, wishing to punish successful development and destroy existing infrastructures because of a mischaracterization of reality.

Suffering is a part of conscious being. You cannot relieve it by destroying things that relieve it, that just makes it worse. There exists no better proof of the State's incompetence at delivering us from suffering than any government program that is aimed at such. Because of Marxist framing, they cannot see their march for power for what it is, a grand game of musical chairs. In each case of history, as new leadership becomes part of the socio-cultural substructures, they become conservative because the worst scenario is to fall from grace, so this becomes their focus. Idealism is moot in the face of power. Idealism is immaterial, and men are not.

CHAPTER NINE:

Liberal Subversion: An Attack on Our Instincts

There is liberalism in many of us, and many see this as harmless or even good, but it is insidious. It tears at our core instincts, and leads us to destruction. We must tear this away from ourselves if we wish our civilization to survive.

Our liberal paradigm seems harmless, but it eats away at the very core of our lives. Like some poisons absorbed in low doses, slowly we build up a certain immunity to its harmful effects, at least in our perception.

But our perception is poisoned. We are not living normal lives when compared to our ancestors: those who survived in order to bring us into being. We accept unacceptable things often without thinking it through, or only shallowly. We then observe the overall results and cannot fathom why society has gone so wrong.

We witness a myriad of ills; we see policy with no productive purpose; we see a failing education system; we see rampant vice and degeneration; yet we look at the state of the system and think: "How could it be so broken?"

By we, I do not necessarily mean "us", or even myself, but rather the collective societal "we", the one which should reflect the greater whole of our nation should it be possible for it to experience cognition as if it were a conscious organism in and of itself. Perhaps that is the problem, and perhaps the corpus callosum of our civilization is what is broken, for surely our right eye watches in awe while the left eye wonders what the hell happened.

For example, even the most liberal of people would choose a female babysitter over a male, and most would actively avoid hiring a homosexual of any stripe for such a job, and trans would be right off the table. Should they not, their instinct has been annihilated. For what better measure can one have of instinct than their willingness to risk their offspring's health and survival? What better measure of evolutionary fitness can one have but their timidity in the face of expulsion from the gene pool?

We may even laugh at the ridiculous things some people do, but what within ourselves is equally laughable? There come many issues that a libertarian-type might hold tightly to, like homosexuality being about consent and tolerance. But what is tolerance but piecemeal timidity in the face of annihilation? Should homosexuals wish to engage in their behaviour, in a private setting and without anyone else knowing, what would it matter? It really does not! But should it be legal, if that fact alone leads to it becoming public knowledge which corrupts the social order into oblivion? Then it must be made illegal! Perhaps it goes too far to enforce that legal status too much, perhaps the over-enforcement is the real problem (for it forces a grievance), but should it not be stopped and stayed from public view, if the alternative is a collapse into widespread degeneration? Who gains from openly public homosexuality exactly? *Cui bono?*

Anyone with a brain sees that the contemporary exposure of the trans lifestyle flowed directly from the opening up to gaydom into the public sphere. Slippery slope aside, the growth of "acceptance" and "tolerance" is not simply people becoming more "enlightened", for all the data says the opposite! Attention spans are drastically down! IQ scores are down 1.5 points per decade on average since the 1870s! People are more attracted to shiny lights and pornography than they are books or relationships. Millions of young men willingly give their money to women on the internet for what? A snowflake's chance in hell to attract her? These young men know hardly anything about attraction. They are effeminate, weak, soy-sodden and juvenile. No. This acceptance and tolerance is the classic sign of a dying civilization: Welcome to the Disenlightenment.

Tolerance should extend to what is not destructive and no further! That should be the limit of our patience! Do not be fooled or cajoled otherwise. The lives of your descendants and their civilization depends on it: millions of people across aeons, who by your failures to recognize the dangers, doom them. What difference is it from suicide? None! It is an infinite Holocaust of the multitudes within you!

Is it kindness to encourage failure or weakness? It is destructive and evil. Yet liberalism promotes this behaviour. Should you feed a drug addict drugs or money for him to get drugs? What if he dies as a result, in order to "cure" his pain? You didn't mean to though! It just happened! Well, nothing "just happens". If you played a role in their death through procurement of that which killed him, how could you not feel guilty? That guilt is the acknowledgment that you did wrong, that your failure in virtue killed someone.

We see it in our lives today. Our nations lurch from crisis to crisis, and with each we learn nothing because we must always lurch. Never can we be allowed to ponder, for that would lead to reflection and then we would have to deny our own part in it. Denial is constructed outside of our view and so when this insidious force finally amasses a real problem, the first thing a liberal must do is deny it exists. For how could it? Problem X is far more prevalent! Focus on that!

We find this sort of thing prominently in the alleged "anti-woke" sphere, in characters like Karlyn Borosenko, James Lindsay, Eric Weinstein, Elon Musk; to some degree as well Jordan Peterson and Bret Weinstein, though I say they are a slightly different category. Jordan and Bret do not march in lockstep to the liberal paradigm, and sometimes their nascent instincts keep them grounded in reality, but they do falter and fall into the subverted liberal default on certain subject matter. Peterson especially should know better, or perhaps he does but is not willing to risk saying it.

There is a certain disdain I have for that, as I think Peterson could take those extra steps, steps he even preaches in his lectures as a necessary component of the maintenance of civilization. At the same time, he is doing a lot of work standing between even more subversive degenerate rhetoric and the soft, flailing masses of normies; and so I fear his piece being removed from the board resulting in something far worse, like brainwashed Normie Progressive Death Squads seeking out the ideologically impure at the barrel of a gun and the zeal backed by powerful weapons and perceived righteousness. Should we lose his piece we would first need to be prepared for Total War, but perhaps I'm just pessimistic.

The promised program of peace and tolerance has not been achieved. Instead we have only had continuous ideological war for over a decade. They are coming hard for your children now. What will you do? Will you tolerate it? Or will you have the moral backbone to shove degeneracy back into the closet whence forth it came?

CHAPTER TEN:

Literacy and the Managerial Bureaucracy:
Managers, Traps, and Propaganda

I was driving in town in early June 2024, and I thought back to a discussion Jordan Peterson had with someone (I can't remember who), where one of the virtues of the illiterate is that they are less easily fooled than most literate people.

I characterize this, on the part of the literate, as their susceptibility to feel charmed by their capacity to interpret meaning from written symbols on a page or screen. Now THEY KNOW the truth comes forth via the sacred symbols and scratchings of wise men long lived, long passed.

How could they be wrong? For indeed this is often true. Often they are absorbing the thoughts of long dead but wiser men, or women, from whom they can glean knowledge so as to be *those who stand upon the shoulders of giants.* But do they?

In many senses, writing is like a proper inoculation which prevents Civilizations from repeating the same mistakes or having to rediscover the same knowledge and information over and over. In this sense it preserves and maintains civilization. But it also has a tendency to act like an open wound, allowing easy access for entropic actors to infect, manipulate, weaken, or destroy its host's mind. Brain infections are essentially the worst case scenario.

Meanwhile the illiterate must be genuinely convinced, cajoled, or made to act in a manner which may violate their protective instinct, a scar-like tissue formed by experience which defends them against nonsense. Such people are accused of being closed-minded. This is often the case, but it is important to understand this defensive mechanism as anti-entropic.

Often they will not move in their position without overwhelming reason, and even then, may still hold out. Some will view this as a halting of *progress* and so liberals have created concepts like *imminent domain* laws which allow the State to take your property for the purposes of some *greater good* and pay the owner the *prevailing market rate*.

To an illiterate, they are being unjustly, unreasonably, and wrongly oppressed by the State, to a point where their long-held familial plot and inheritance for their children has been stolen. But to a literate, they have been treated fairly by a nearly sacred and unassailable law and writ. In fact, by merely calling it the law, it is right by a literate person, and they will even participate in the violence necessary to see the law through.

But who makes those laws? Or better yet, who applies those laws? Bureaucrats. They come in many forms: Police, Politicians, Office workers, managers, judges, lawyers; all of them bureaucrats, and all of them possessing their own priorities and goals within the framework of the power system.

This framework is designed for a number of purposes, mainly the distribution of power and responsibility. But who is in charge of metering out such things? The bureaucrats themselves. What is the result? Policy which leads to favourable outcomes and protections for bureaucrats. So where does the responsibility part come in? Here is the neat part for the bureaucrat: *as far away from the managerial bureaucracy as possible.*

This is the defining aspect of power in Western democracy, the denial of responsibility, or to direct responsibility onto anything else. How is this done? Media Communications and Public Relations. This of course requires that the population be generally literate. After that, power can maintain itself indefinitely until it becomes incompetent.

The general public isn't generally willing to question the motives or actions of power, because power lies beyond them. It is merely an entity which does stuff, sometimes you need to pay it money or fines. Sometimes it punishes "bad guys". It helps all the more that systems have been implemented in order to extract wealth from the normal person, via things like payroll direct taxes, sales taxes, fees on services.

All of these are considered "legitimate" by the public due to the *democratic process* in which the public are allowed to choose their representatives who then work for the people. But the truth is, that these representatives are then corralled into paddocks and forced to make set decisions because, *if you don't make the expert recommendation, you will be held responsible*. But again, who is held responsible for those decisions when they turn out badly? Always the elected representative. The bureaucracy remains essentially intact.

It won't matter either because the media will eat the politician alive, excoriate them to the public who will, being previously cajoled into general agreeability, now lacking their natural scepticism, will go along with it. It will be a ceaseless force against change, which of course only heightens the ever-growing crisis of competency in the power system.

This is unsustainable. There needs to be room for change. There needs to be space to alter course and not be forced to watch our society drive the ship of State over Niagara Falls. The bureaucracy will drive us over this edge if we do not exercise discerning scepticism of it.

Blind adherence should be reserved for faith, not governance. Render unto Caesar that which is Caesar's; render unto God that which is God's. Currently Canada and much of the West is experiencing a crisis of faith in our political systems, a faith we never should have ever had. Our previously waning scepticism needs to be kicked into full gear. You should have NO faith in the bureaucratic system.

The challenge now is the public relations concept. How do we disable its grip on the literate? Literacy should have value, but I believe that it has been twisted into something it never should have been.

It is true that most people in the West are literate. It is also true that most in the West read NOTHING at all of any value. The writing of average people comes across as garbled nonsense, even after twelve years of compulsory education! So what do most people read when they bother to? People might say important things like stop signs, the newspaper, warnings on tobacco products or even nutritional labels on food products. The truth is that no one reads those. Have you ever met a smoker who quit because of the disgusting pictures on the cartons?

So what are they reading? What use is literacy then? Many read fiction, previous to the C-19 era around 50% of the population would read one book per year. During C-19 this increased to about 64%, and has been slumping back to the earlier level. More apparently read non-fiction, but one must consider the density or relevance of these.

Anything outside of the power paradigm is difficult to publish, whether or not it is true. Who controls publishing? The managerial bureaucracy. Not completely of course, but managers will not risk a chance to move up the ladder, and if publishing a no-no book threatens that, they will play it safe and decline. In any case, this creates a pressure against truly dissenting voices from being spread too widely.

So again, what are they reading? They are mostly reading managerial-approved works, if they are reading at all. Outside of that? *Advertising? Journalism? Propaganda?* What is happening to journalists who have challenged power recently? When they challenge a particular politician it seems to be a coin flip. But when it comes to challenging the institutions of the managerial system (MBS), it is essentially a *death sentence* in one way or another. Is there any virtue in reading advertising? No.

So what is left outside of receiving letters from family or friends (rare), reading social media (empty) honestly I couldn't think of many more that the average person would come across other than the aforementioned and the following: Instructions and demands from the MBS; documents from the MBS; direct propaganda from the MBS.

It is true that some read research papers and such which are becoming easier to access, but this is by far in the minority and even if you were to read them, you would be powerless in the face of the MBS to compete in your viewpoint on the conclusions, as the public relations bureau would easily outcompete you for both messaging, airtime, and breadth.

But wait! There is more! In the MBS you have "free speech/expression", right? Except you don't. It certainly says you do in the basic reading of the Charter of Rights and Freedoms (Canada), or the First Amendment (USA). But in Canada you have this thing called Section One. Originally this was put in for *"State-Threatening National Emergencies where the territorial and existential integrity of Canada was at stake"*, but has since been used as an excuse to suppress Canadian speech and expression.

The Courts which were purposed to uphold law and order, have determined that speech and expression must be limited, because certain expression and speech might go against peace and good government, or threaten the rights of others. Often this is the "maximal free expression" argument, which claims that by oppressing some views, it increases the free expression of other views. In other words, the Courts in Canada have come up with a zero-sum concept of expression. This is of course entirely illogical, because no matter how much Party A expresses their views, it will never impinge on the volume of expression for Party B (assuming neither are directly interfering with each other, and should the courts favour one set of views over another, that is direct interference in expression anyways).

This has led me to come to the conclusion that the Charter in

Canada is not a set of rights and freedoms, but rather a managerial document meant to express ideal conditional exceptions which can be taken away at any point based on managerial immediacy. If convenient to the regime and power, you may have "rights". Thus the entirety of the Charter, outside of Section One, is *Advisory*. The document is, whether by its nature or by its interpretation, Managerial and malicious. It lies to the general public and proudly proclaims how free and empowering it is, while stomping upon the heads of anyone who takes such a proclamation seriously. Since the number of people who will actively use the Charter as it is presented is quite low, the MBS has no problem containing dissident thought, as the few foolish flies caught in its webs are exsanguinated and disposed of heartlessly through the various soul-crushing processes which only a Bureaucrat could conjure up.

So how do we solve this? First I think we need to take a page from the State and diminish the value of the Charter, at least to help protect innocent people from becoming victims of regime oppression through their traps. This will require an expansion of criticism of the Charter, and paper rights in general. The regime needs also to be criticized over its lack of responsibility for its decision making apparatuses, and the unimpeachable Managerial Bureaucracy. The consensus mechanisms of the MBS also need to be criticized and, ideally, shattered into a million pieces, at least in terms of public perception.

This process of MBS growth is a Stage Four Cancer in our society. As far as I can see, there is no cure. It will require the building of new institutions which must compete for legitimacy in the public view. In the end there need be no violent conflict, as the MBS will eventually self-destruct. However, it may lash out in its death-throes, so this will need to be prepared for, out of a need for survival of society as a whole, and for no other reason. Step carefully, friends.

CHAPTER ELEVEN:

Meaning: Becoming, Establishing, Reproduction, and Legacy

We are interesting creatures, without a doubt. Joseph Campbell once said man is a strange mix of animal and God, that we have our heads in the clouds and our feet in the dirt. Our minds can however be blinded by these clouds and sometimes forget about our feet, our place in being.

At the same time this blindness encourages us to seek meaning in our lives, imagining our reality as a tale playing out before us with a beginning, middle, and end. Sometimes this comes in the form of the seasons we witness throughout the year, and in the ways in which we feel the cycles of the day and night. Like the ticking of a clock, we pace through time, in moments of astonishment, banality, and depression. But what is the point of all that, and what does it take to get from one end to the other, successfully? And why?

Why is an important question, and it is the origin for this piece. Many reading this don't know their roots, their heritage; that which anchors them to the Great Chain of Being. I come from a long line of people who left their homes on the European continent; some first sons but many second or third sons looking to find the space to author their own epoch. They went out and conquered uncivilized lands and built our world which we are so blessed to enjoy. This is true for most of us in America (both the USA and *the rest*). But now we are in a crisis of *meaning*, because we have *forgotten*. It is high time that we started to *remember* who we are.

We strain for meaning in our lives, and many of us break in the process. Let it not be unsaid, many of our lives are completely wasted. People move forward without pursuit, living what I feel is an animal life... only they are NOT animals. They feel this meaninglessness in their being, they know something is not right about their lives. But what? Where do we go wrong in our pursuit of this? How are so many lost along the way? I will break this into four sections, each building upon each other into a totality of "meaning". These sections are: Becoming, Establishing, Reproduction, and Legacy.

Becoming-

There is no being without becoming. The foundation of your birth is the fundamental relationship between your parents, their parents, and the rest of your ancestry. In short we call this heritage. Many denounce a call to heritage as a "dog whistle" or "old thinking", but this is nonsense.

Heritage must come before you are born, and although it is not necessary to go very far back for it to be a useful foundation of meaning, it must be understood. The further you can recall your ancestry, the better. But I define "lost heritage" as a person who didn't know any of their four grandparents, and I define it having been partially lost if none of that person's grandparents knew a single one of their own grandparents. Now, why?

Grandchildren are the legacy of grandparents. Their children, in contrast, are the products of parents. Direct products are of course important, but they carry a different quality than the products of the products, which indicates an established legacy, demonstrating the subject having, through their being, left a lasting effect upon the world.

Birth is the next most important part of meaning, for without it, there is no being. As the product of your parents, the qualities of their own individual establishment will affect you, and will determine portions of your being. In many ways birth and heritage are synonymous as you do not have memories of very early childhood, yet they form the basis of what makes you, you, rather than someone else.

We must grow. Growth is a layer in our life's meaning and there are few creatures who are disrespected more than infantile adults. This is growth in the physical sense, and additionally in the sense of emotional and psychological maturation and development. Is the child sociable? Is the child learning about the world and themselves? Are they making progress towards personal independence and capacity? Did you as a child maximize your growth potential through your own efforts? Did you have enough support?

Support, or education, comes in many forms. Manners, expectations, discipline and balance, all play a role in your development as a person. Balance is equally important to all the other concepts mentioned, because the difference between obsession and interest is one of degree. The difference between discipline and abuse is a matter of control versus a lack of control (itself a lack of proper discipline). The same can be said of manners and expectations, for when either is adhered to in an extreme manner, it produces a stiffness in attitude and sometimes self-destructive behaviour. Translated further, becoming quickly blends into establishing, which is a layer we build towards.

Establishing-

Building upon education is the development of skills. Ideally these skills are useful in life and not merely masturbatory in nature. This builds towards marketability, which brings confidence, allowing one to build themselves up into something useful for both their family and society.

This marketability and usefulness allows a person to make deeper connections to others, layering the social with the economic, ripening relationships, and in so doing, strengthening their sense of self, their sense of belonging to something greater than themselves, and their sense of meaning. Someone in this state will find transitioning from the productive self into the reproductive self, very natural.

Reproduction-

Transitioning from a productive self into the reproductive

self builds upon the previously established meaning one has developed. In order to reproduce, one requires a mate, and the ability to attain one requires many of the earlier developed skills, such as sociability, balance, confidence, marketability, and health. Courting is the display of oneself as an embodiment of these things, while seeking out another who will compliment these characteristics.

The goal of course doesn't need to be said, though many aim for marriage. Once mated, this relationship typically produces offspring, establishing a permanent heritage in common for these children. It must be stressed that in choosing a mate, you are not only choosing them, but their whole family, their whole heritage, to be shared with yours. Many misunderstand this aspect of marriage, but it is true. You are intertwining your legacies via reproduction.

In doing this, you have taken on the task of imbuing your offspring with your experience, skills, knowledge, wealth, circumstance, being, and meaning. Your children will be the foundation of your legacy, and how you impact them will directly impact whatever you hope to leave behind that is good, or bad, in the world.

Legacy-

The pinnacle of meaning, it might be said, is what you can look back upon and know you have left behind. It is the impact of your life's being, the wake of your keel upon the waters of life. The accumulation of love, hate, forgiveness, contempt, failure and redemption, all rolled into one teary-eyed splendour. The unexamined life is not worth living, it is said, but what does that mean? Do you look back on your life fondly? Knowingly? Or do you turn your head from the past, avert your eyes, and say "I cannot look upon it, no more, NO MORE!"? Was all your suffering worthwhile? Was your hard journey fruitful? For some, to look back on their lives is very painful. If you always live in the now, there is a reason.

Such a wince of pain, not for physical injury, but mental

anguish, merciless, the kind which damns you to suffer without abatement. A sort of torture to the point of tedious delirium where the past no longer exists, for every moment you remember it is like a knife carving at your soul. For many this will drive them to drink. And can we blame them at that point? Yes. But I understand why they self-destroy, for their meaning is nothing. They have no legacy. It is as though they never existed, and they feel it! What impact did they make? perhaps some, but who will remember? Sure, some can leave behind a legacy that didn't come forth through their loins, but very few manage. The crisis of meaning does not emanate from our great inventors and visionaries, but from the average, everyday Joe. Failing to warn young people of this is criminal; it is a bewitching trick and travesty sending men to their spiritual ruin. As Dostoyevsky notes in the Brothers Karamazov, the worst sin is to destroy and betray yourself, for nothing.

Legacy, as I stated earlier, is your grandchildren. They are the physical embodiment of your work and heritage combined into being itself. Your role then is enrichment, endowment, presence, gratefulness, mutuality, and encouragement. These children of your children are your love letters to the future. They represent both the culmination of your selflessness, and the physical embodiment of your sacrifice. They are the proof of the meaning within your life's work and being. If you desire meaning, then let nothing stop you.

CHAPTER TWELVE:

The Boomer Cruise: a Faustian Fingertrap

The Day of the Pillow

A spectre is haunting Europe – the spectre of traditionalism. All the powers of GloboHomo have entered into an unholy alliance to exorcise this spectre: Pope and President, Managers and intelligentsia, French Radicals and German police spies.

Where is the party in opposition that has not been decried as regressive by its opponents in power? Where is the opposition that has not hurled back the branding reproach of traditionalism, against the conservative opposition parties, as well as against its progressive adversaries?

Two things result from this fact:

I. Traditionalism is already acknowledged by all GloboHomo powers to be itself a power.

II. It is high time that Traditionalists should openly, in the face of the whole world, publish their views, their aims, their tendencies, and meet this nursery tale of the Spectre of Traditionalism with a manifesto of the idea itself.

History is always a conflict between the visions of progress and the reality of historical cycles.

In history, we find almost everywhere a complicated arrangement of society into various orders, a manifold gradation of social rank. In ancient Rome we have patricians, knights, plebeians, and slaves; in the Middle Ages, feudal lords, vassals, guild-masters, journeymen, apprentices, and serfs; in almost all of these classes, again, subordinate gradations. These graduations and classifications were orderly and stabilizing for society, bringing it great wealth and knowledge.

Modern society has sprouted from the ruins of feudal society; modernity bastardizes many traditional concepts and subverts them for commercialization, and has established new classes, new conditions, and new forms of struggle in place of the former.

Our epoch, the epoch of GloboHomo, possesses, however, this distinct feature: it has simplified Society as a whole by splitting people up into hostile camps, into near-infinite microcosms, forced to hate each other or absorb the bug-man spirit.

From the serfs of the Middle Ages sprang the chartered burghers of the earliest towns. From these burgesses, the first elements of GloboHomo were developed.

The discovery of America, and the rounding of the Cape, opened up fresh ground for the rising managerial class. The East Indian and Chinese markets, the colonization of America, trade with the colonies, and the increase in the means of exchange and commodities generally, gave to commerce, navigation, to industry, an impulse never before known, and thereby, to the revolutionary element in the tottering feudal society, a rapid development.

The feudal system of industry, in which industrial production was monopolized by closed guilds, now no longer sufficed for the growing wants of the new markets. The manufacturing system took its place. The guild masters were pushed to one side by the manufacturing middle class; the division of labour between the different corporate guilds vanished in the face of the division of labour in every single workshop.

Meantime the markets kept ever growing, the demand ever rising. Even manufacturers no longer sufficed. Thereupon, steam and machinery revolutionized industrial production. The place of manufacture was taken by the giant, Modern Industry; the place of the industrial middle class by industrial millionaires, the leaders of the whole industrial armies, and the modern manager.

Modern industry has established the world market, for which the discovery of America paved the way. This market has given an immense development to commerce, navigation, and communication by land. This development has, in its turn, reacted to the extension of industry; and in proportion as industry, commerce, navigation, and railways extended; in the same proportion GloboHomo developed, increased its capital, and pushed into the background every tradition handed down from the Middle Ages.

A Precursor

We thus arrive at postmodernity, which, whether defined by or not, has catered to the Boomer. The nascent radical of the 1960s (having been largely born in the late 1940s and 1950s) had grown up in a world that treated them as Princely producers for the world crushed by War. There was no shortage of work mending a world so broken by bloodshed, and they did some but soon sold the ancient silver long kept in the familial cupboards for the sinking hole of individuality. The Boomer began to cruise.

Cruising began in youth, easy-come jobs and historically high wages led to many boomers having cars in high school. Driving tests were easy, with learner's permits only being needed for a handful of weeks. In this way many would drive around town, getting into "trouble", looking cool in their 1960s-1970s land-boats with fuel as cheap as chips. Life was great from their point of view.

Then, social accomplishment was simple. But soon the boomer females too became "empowered", and though they held some traditional aspects of civilization within their hearts, they soon became feral; a certain madness overcame the lot of them. Civilization declined.

Many boomers married young, for whatever reason, (often out of expectations, or style) and many of these relationships lasted some 20 years or more, usually producing 2 or more children. Suddenly, there is invented this idea of a mid-life crisis, which gave boomers the idea they could restart their lives with a new partner in their late 30s or 40s. For many boomers, marriage was not a holy union making up the foundation of civilization to the benefit of their offspring, but a socio-economic symbol of prestige worn somewhat like the war medals of their fathers.

With this, many women had no choice but to take up employment outside of the home for economic survival, which was no longer a stable platform with which to build a happy life, but a fleeting moment of cruising, never knowing when the ship would weigh anchor and send you off to the nearest port to explore unknown reaches of captured, designed, and curated pastures where you can wade through the artificial grass.

This subversion of the natural order, this indoctrination into industrial-centric living, is all-consuming. It devours vast swathes of humanity: mentally in terms of thought; physically in terms of effort; existentially in terms of being or being born. Why have a family when you are satiated by mass-manufacturing? That is essentially what is fed into our minds through advertising and other propaganda. It is by the grace of God that many have children at all. Pure instinct or happenstance, running on the fumes of nature that remains in Man. Contemporary propaganda informs you that this world is too expensive to procreate, at the moment in history when life has never been easier.

Cruisin' for a Bruisin'

But it stems from this: the Boomer Cruise. Boomers will stop at nothing, short of having nothing left, to Cruise. Many plan to leave nothing to their heirs but a mass of credit card bills, a home-equity loan, lines of credit and much more! "Après moi le déluge" they seem to say, as they burn through their assets just in time to have none when they expire. Typical of Boomer

Cruising, is travelling on cruise ships on the open ocean to various spots, getting drunk on board, or going to all-inclusive resorts like in Mexico or the Mediterranean. This much-differentiates from Pilgrimage, or voyages of discovery. These are indulgent, masturbatory excursions suited to the aspirations of the lower classes who would do better by trying to get their family ahead than travelling across the continent to…be warm while outside. Don't get me wrong of course! What's not to love about a nice romp down in Mexico or Spain? But if this is how you soothe your bio-spiritual yearnings, my friend, swallow deep on that blue pill because that's all for which you are capable.

This is of course not to blend all boomers into one socioeconomic smooth-brained stew, for many boomers are active in intergenerational wealth planning. But it should be indicative of where you are placed within the rungs of humanity. Many however do work merely so they can have their head hit that pillow each night, in a cycle that has them working to sleep. Dare to awaken them, thinking you can change them and you might permanently join them. Comfort is a commodity, but its cost is impoverishment. You can become addicted to comfort, the greatest of all drugs. To wit, what is a drug but a seeking of refuge in the name of comfort? What is it to be high but to escape the bondages of material being, mortal suffering, even if just for a moment of peace? An addict will pay nearly any price, do nearly any deed, to attain this! Such energy and gumption, all put to the cause of self-destruction.

Wrestling the Shadowy Darkness

The Boomer Cruise is not merely a problem because it seeks out masturbatory indulgences, but because it seeks out *death*. It is a slow, painful, cultural suicide. The existence of communities relies on the existence of traditions, ceremonies, festivals and other things which bring the community together in collective orchestrations, aspiring towards a unity of folk and purpose. To lead in any direction which diminishes or ignores such held truths is to stab at them with knives of falsehoods. It is to lynch the very basis upon which being resides, in the continuous cycling of the generations, celebrating life and renewal, mourning the dead and from their honourable lives heroes and legends abound, beyond the material reality of their long-buried bones.

Despite this, our ruins, these ashes where our faint hopes trod, hope remains in us. You can reflect upon the failures of the Boomer Cruise and drive your course to the promised land. You must shed your own internal boomer lies and logic, you must be willing to lift the veil and dash through to the other side. Ever-thinning strands hold together the dilapidated structures of civilization. In Europe there is more hope than most, for the strands are still graspable, should you reach out and have them.

But for the New Worlders, beyond some Novo-Hyperborean fever dream, you must dig deep, and you must cast aside the subversions plaguing you. If there is nothing to you but sportsball and statutory holidays, you are in a bad way. If you have nothing, you must create something, anything, and make it last. European Man and Colonials alike, the Bureaucracy has you by your throats, and holds you weakly, while the technocracy works at your castration. Do not be meek at this moment! Do not sleep while they slice at your God-given gonads! Do what you must so that your progeny lives on! You have everything to lose; your children need you and without your will to act their existence fades into obscurity. They will never have the choice, unless you can make yours. Which way, European Man?

CHAPTER THIRTEEN:

On Fortune: Lament

It is said that fortune favours the bold, but why would someone believe that? Is it courage which fortune favours? No. It is the will to act when the moment announces itself through the fog of abstraction and into perception. Fortune, she arrives in many forms, but many do not act, not merely due to cowardice but due to impropriety, unreadiness, and unwillingness. Fortune is neither a shield nor a sword, but a moment of time. Boldness births forth from this as the will to act on the moment and seize the advantage so generously lent to such an actor. For time, it passes us by like a raging river, with us sheltered by the shore, unmoving, frozen stiff in fear of the destructive currents.

That is life. The torrent never ceases but waxes and wanes like the moon, presenting moments of both superior brightness and clarity, and utter darkness and obscurity. Choosing not to act is easy, and gives the impression of security. But we all know that floods happen and wash entire peoples to their deaths; so to not act in any manner is to invite death to your door to have its way with you. So can inaction be said to be security? No, it cannot be. There is never any security other than that which is provided through one's own acts of will and self ownership, and the continual possession of one's own liberty. But what instruction can we gain in order to know when to act and how to act?

No man as man currently is, was born into a vacuum; for if he were he would never require action, he would have perished immediately. All men are born into a culture, a society, a family. Each is endowed with an essential narrative, and if he is not then he is doomed to a path of hellish destruction. He who struggles forth without a narrative does so to the effect of his own ruin, and although one might attest that he went to ruin, it cannot be said that he ever lived, and so therefore never died. He became undone by his own lack of direction like a naive explorer of parts unknown, doomed to the labyrinth of the world. Untold fathoms of enormous bounty and wealth could not rescue him from his fate, save for an endowment of a narrative compass. Wealth is gained and spent like raindrops in your palms stretched forth in empty hopes of a salvationary gulp of satiation, but the chalice can never be filled because the chalice isn't there. Inasmuch as one without a map survives, he sips these desperate drips in the midst of rushing torrents and rainstorms and barely gets on with being. Each day presents a new struggle for survival wherein a man cannot hope to grasp tertiary thoughts. He is at the mercy of the storm of being, a man thrown overboard by his culture who failed to teach him how to sail (or perhaps he refused to learn, as some men are evidently fated!)

Fortune favours the bold, but not those who are adrift. How do you know if you are adrift or at sail in your narrative mapping of the world? How many rocks can your hopes and dreams upon be dashed before you yearn for the painless sleep of the cold depths below? How long must you endure the Leviathan's lament of his defeat by the Almighty? The ultimate externalization of the protagonist slew it with prejudice and cast it into the depths in disgrace, for it to rise again in opposition in a never-ending battle of will against submission. But what of that protagonist you project? Are you not a protagonist in your own narrative? One answer is a resounding yes, whilst the alternative is death.

As individuals one must know that they possess the potential to live, and therefore exist as a protagonist in their own narrative reality. Inasmuch as they choose to live they exist as this protagonist. However, inasmuch they choose not to live, they exist as antagonists to themselves and aim the self towards doom. This is a fundamental and therefore inescapable truth. Many deny this about themselves, yet it remains just as true regardless. We instead blame outside forces for our conditions without reference to what condition OUR own condition is in. We are not passive beings in this life, we choose to live, or we don't. Our actions determine which is true. This element of being, our own self-antagonism, is fully and utterly under the spell of our own will. Any other concept is to reduce our responsibility for our condition, and in doing so we are reducing our being itself in reference to itself. To externalize our antagonism is to choose death over living, to go forth in cowardice towards the darkness, and be completely enveloped therein, delivered as an act of will into the welcoming embrace of the Leviathan.

The path to redemption lay not within a pilgrimage to some holy site, nor does it lay within a magic spell or ritual, but in the acknowledgement of will, and the seeking of the will to live. We cannot allow ourselves to be tempted by the will to death, to the suicide of spirit. We cannot revive the Leviathan into a creative union in order for it to do our bidding, for its purpose is to destroy. It is the element of unbeing, and no hopes exist of it resurfacing via the collective unwill of spiritual sleepwalkers. The sword cannot be wielded by the armless dead, but the living may attempt to raise it from its lair (even though such an act would be to commit to unbeing). But a Pandora's Box of woes be unto those who wield such a weapon. Hope alone will be all that remains for salvation under such a circumstance, for all is not lost if Hope remains. But of this Hope, one must embrace still further this will to live.

It is within the darkest times and moments of great obscurity where our only refuge is hope, that is to say the will to live on, the active choice to persist. To boldly hold the line against the cold embrace of oblivion untold. Many foresee the Leviathan coming and therein surrender to its magnanimity for they cannot withstand its force within their own hearts. Fallacy! The will is great! Immense! It is greater than the Leviathan! Will itself the size of a mustard seed can move mountains of mountains, the

Leviathan stands no chance against even a lone man with the will to persist, to live, to oppose the Leviathan and the immediate embrace of oblivion! Oblivion comes for us all one day but not yet today! One must say it to its face with a heroic heart, blessed with will. Never mind the measure of the beast, never mind the measure of the man, be it only for will to decide fate, he devours the Leviathan and lays him below, damned, beyond the abyssal plain on which our fortunes grow.

CHAPTER FOURTEEN:

The Problem with Regulation: Incompetent & Hubristic Bureaucrats

Theoretically regulation brings security, protects nature, human beings, and animals. However, complications arising from regulation are ignored.

Regulations attempt to provide security at liberty's debit. This *cannot* be regained until it's repealed or is de facto ignored. This exchange is farcical, because such security is farcical. Power capable of ensuring security itself becomes a precarity: true security lies in liberty.

The State's claim fails. It instead offers "resolution". State-security is reactive, and attempts to resolve damages post-facto. It shows "strength" at airports, Parliament, Congress, and the like. Post-September 11th 2001, airport security expanded sparing no expense. Has it helped? Terrorists have never been caught through it. I personally feel no security going through, as do many others, and feel instead that my own liberty is simply abused. Bureaucracy again expands to meet the needs of the expanding bureaucracy, parasitizing the State.

Industrial regulation hampers productivity, competitiveness, innovation, efficiency, and *trust.* It's a redistribution of resources to soothe the State's penchant for violence. The effect upon consumers is increased price due to increase in cost, and lowered production from decreased efficiency. Regulations are inflationary as they reduce market competitiveness through higher capital expense, restrained innovation, and weakened entrepreneurship.

Regulations benefit larger established firms, and pressure monopolization which harms consumers, productivity, technological development, and even State security, (which relies on taxation) thus, not only does regulation create direct negative effects, it fails at the task to which it's purposed.

"Liability" could be the solution: relying on private agencies trading in risk, merchants would be obliged to contain liability through capital reserves of their own, or by contracting risk to an insurer. This is the purpose of insurance.

Courts rule on liability. Insurance providers and precedent-based Law could require monitoring for potential risks. If there are releases or damages, the monitoring could determine guilt. The Law might set precedent such that lack of monitoring is negligence (this is already common).

Through monitoring, damages are apportioned, punishing negligence and rewarding responsibility. Self-monitoring protects oneself, which is in anyone's interest. Insurers can refuse service if customers fail standards. Without insurance, investors are unlikely to risk capital buying shares, essentially hampering business growth.

An example: "Mining Co." has a mine carrying risks of $1 Billion; operations require liability funding. After capital expenditures it doesn't have $1 Billion. Without insurance, their capital expenditures are risked, harming shareholder value. They contract with insurer, "Moramony Co." which evaluates the risks and informs "Mining Co" that by mitigating risks, through better equipment, document keeping and training, the risk of a $1 billion accident occurs once per 1000 years. They calculate that it'll cost the insurer $1,000,000 annually to guarantee liability coverage and offer liability coverage for $2,000,000 annually. "Mining Co." shops around to determine if it's fair. The insurer uses this money to create a pool of capital for management and expenditures. The insurer increases their rates for clients who violate the standards or cease coverage to those who are risky.

This creates a relationship where each party has interest in best results. Firms know coverage entices investors, increasing its value.

If damages occur the damaged party is compensated. In the case of pollutants, courts take in class action suits, which could be simplified, with the accused firms having to prove their due diligence/innocence via monitoring. Damages are paid by offenders proportional to their contribution. Failure in due diligence monitoring could be punished more severely, damages multiplied to incentivize compliance. Mechanisms need to assure that injured parties are genuine before a case can move forward.

Over time courts would create a common-law through case-law to determine limitations of suits. Perhaps light smoke from a BBQ isn't prosecutable but pollution from a power plant demonstrates compensable injury.

Regulations make the State an insurance company, liability laying with taxpayers. The State charges fees, runs inspections, and enforces rules, but there's no interest from the parties. Industry skirts rules to the limits. They may get a warning. Shareholders are safe, because taxpayers cover liability. The State doesn't care if it fails, because they can always milk taxpayers for money. Meanwhile they get "free" money from industry to bankroll causes helping politicians campaign. But when things fail, the company collapses, damages remain, becoming the problem of the neighbours and taxpayers. Politicians disappear, and new ones arise and make promises. Regulations are rebranded, and the process repeats. The taxpayer holds the bag and all future bags: limited only by bag-holding tolerance.

In commerce there's no greater enemy than regulation. Money is an abstraction of value. It is a *medium of exchange* enabling greater complexity of transaction, eliminating the problem of requiring a coincidence of needs between parties. Money becomes an easily transported universal medium which holds value over time for reliable trade.

The problem with money is that whoever prints money can counterfeit more to extract or manipulate its value. This affects prices, and destroys savings. It's the fact that currency is an abstraction of value (and not worth anything on its own), which makes it a weapon wielded against anyone without non-liquid capital assets or investments (the vast majority of working people). Socialists claim this is the fault of "Capitalism", but this is false: it's a manipulation by force (or trickery). It has nothing to do with Capitalism, but the Government.

If a currency doesn't maintain stability over time, users lacking non-liquid capital assets won't attain capital or assets, as they are stuck chasing inflation. Non-liquid capital assets don't just disappear. We know where the wealth goes. The inflationary loss experienced by the working class transfers in the form of inflationary gain to the banks through initializing loans to which they receive a privileged status by the State, Central Bank and mints. This liquidity is laundered through the economy, but was not initially calculated in the market. As it works through to the consumer level, it's "realized" and the value of money falls relative to consumer goods. The consumer suffers reduced purchasing power.

The guilt is on the State, for it allows for counterfeiting. This problem exists in all systems using central banking willing to manipulate money. The State never acknowledges the problem. Instead, it promotes itself as the cure! It regulates to solve the problems it first creates through its meddling, and then says it can solve it through further meddling. But let's move onto the specifics of commercial regulation.

Creating entry barriers raises the bar for participation and excludes. Free markets present no entry barrier. Participants are fated by their merits. There's no need for State involvement. Engaging in free market commerce, one comes across the honest and dishonest. The keen soon learn who is worthwhile. The value in the market is figuring out who is and isn't trustworthy, which only happens with markets with free association and dissociation. High trust societies develop from markets that are more free. It's necessary to have a system of law to prevent unlawful uses of force.

But enforcement shouldn't prevent bad deals which encourages the sufferer to disassociate from dishonest people, leading to their marginalization. It'll eventually be true that people are poor and stay poor because of their bad reputation. Since the system rewards good faith actors, there's always opportunity for redemption. The children of dishonest people can be plucked from poverty through being honest to escape the cycle of poverty. The problem is that a parent who is dishonest will often raise their child similarly, endowing them with resentment. Tragic, but not the fault of market economics, but human weakness. This is why meritocracy is important; it gathers the best and brightest of people and rewards them for honesty while marginalizing the dishonest who are disempowered.

Who to trust? Through trial and error. When society loses its base trust it becomes conservative, initiating checks and balances before taking chances. Increased education and training minimums show reluctance to train someone on-the-job. This creates social problems because more resources are invested in order to lower risks for employers. Employees turn to investing heavily in education and training, which employees want to protect, leading to labour regulations, further enforcement mechanisms, higher costs and lower efficiency.

The State only cares about its perpetuation. It doesn't care whatever shape of government it takes. It doesn't care about your freedom, or how much debt it takes on in your name. You can see a small loss of trust has us sprinting towards a massive state bureaucracy, over-bloated education institutions delivering diminishing returns to workers, while failing to reward honest people and marginalize dishonest people. It's a trajectory leading to a loss of liberty, trust, and efficiency.

Regulations don't work. It'll be painful to end them, but in the medium to long term we'll be rewarded. The model is found in every successful developing society. India went from a command economy to a free market economic boom. Socialist China had a relatively free market as well (though this has recently been changing, and will hurt their development).

The Western world is losing the social trust which was our engine of success. We have accomplished this through our good intentions. We created 'rules' and 'standards' to bring about security, and ended up fencing ourselves off from opportunity. Human interaction moves constantly. Decreasing flexibility puts us behind. Nothing is guaranteed by limiting productivity, and leaves us vulnerable.

Regulations won't protect us from the world. We can only imprison ourselves from reality. This is destructive naïveté. There's no entitlement to success, only struggle. Being coddled leaves us slaves. When justice fails what recourse remains? None. We're punished for our weakness, even if we're good. In the end we must fund this bureaucracy that the State has built, which could be avoided if we weren't such cowards.

With healthcare the conversation usually gets stuck on whether or not it's a human right, *who* should bear the costs, and to *what* ends should it be provided. These discussions are thought-provoking. It's undeniable that humans need healthcare to live a healthy life, and it's also undeniable that imperfect medical treatment is superior to an absence of medical treatment (so long as the Hippocratic oath is followed: "If I cannot heal the patient, I will at least do them no harm."). But regulations set the bar high. This creates a monopoly backed by State violence to punish honest practitioners treating patients. If honest people entering the system violate the rules they will be punished. This alone harms people who would've received care. This reduces consumer choice and reduces options for treatment. This "security" could be acquired peacefully through insurance companies and liability.

Practitioners seeking credibility could submit to a private authority on skill, for insurance. This would be voluntary, having the job of approving or disapproving practitioners or rating service providers like Yelp. Different agencies would compete to keep them honest (trust in a rating agency would be paramount to its utility, legitimate practitioners would work to gain the approval of more legitimate ratings agencies). Eventually these ratings agencies would be able to categorize practitioners and so consumers would be able to better judge who to seek out for remedy. This lowers the bar of entry for consumers, meaning the real availability of healthcare increases. The false availability presented by Governments is similar to holding a cow at gunpoint to increase milk production.

The next point is on welfare. People know there are people who can't provide for themselves. But solutions are debatable. The State wants to provide for these people through taxing workers and distributing a portion to those in need. But the disabled, orphaned and elderly have always existed. What was done prior? We had poor houses, orphanages, and hospitals funded by charity. This was done through donations of money, property, or services; sometimes directed through religious orders.

These systems were run by humans not bureaucrats. They weren't based on entitlement, but instead on the values of both the giver and receiver, a mutual understanding of good faith and gratefulness. It tried to not take advantage of others' good faith. Charitable people wouldn't donate to those capable of working, but the State welfare system fills with it. The truly needy are underserved by the State because the dishonest are over-served. With charity there was direct accountability on the part of the receivers, who were grateful for the resources they were given. Can that be said of ours?

Any system using resources inefficiently will fail, because the costs are unsustainable. All costs are borne by society, regardless of source. The costs may not be immediate. As the market "calculates" its resources, production, and distribution all becomes accounted for. Delays of the inevitable come at additional cost. The information is calculated completely, but due to bad information it makes bad decisions, leading to lower efficiency, which leads to increased costs where it was avoidable.

Income tax punishes productivity, property tax punishes property ownership, and sales tax punishes consumption. Governments use all three and more. All taxes punish action, and incentivizes work in grey markets, black markets, or bartering. Welfare incentivizes inaction, non-production, and a sense of entitlement; recipients being generally ungrateful, always demanding more.

Welfare is a deadweight systemic loss. Productive people drag the unproductive. As the welfare system grows, productive people lose tolerance, feeling overburdened by the lazy, unproductive underclass. The eventual collapse of the welfare system will be difficult, and will leave recipients vulnerable. It'll be the fault of the free-riders who are taking advantage of statists helping them. Each productive person dropping into the welfare system is that much more a deceleration of development. The truth is that welfare is worse than charity, as those who cannot afford to give simply don't, and those who can afford to give are rewarded with gratefulness.

Taxation is a burden you cannot escape, a serfdom you cannot break, an entitlement you suffer to remove, for there's no moral limitation like there is in religious endeavours.

The sham cannot last. It's a truth that we must confront. Mankind isn't perfect. We're fallen. The best hope is using the tools available to build a better life, but must come from us. No coercion will make man 'good'. Man is good if it serves his interests. This is experience-based. Regulation is the Babelian fool attempting refutation of God and the perfection of Man. It's a *faithless abomination*, doomed.

That being said, there are times when it should be done, regardless.

CHAPTER FIFTEEN:

Traditionalism in the Postmodern Era: a Treatise

Traditionalism. What is it? What if it's set aside, to fail in its function and form? The tidal forces of time and culture, the ebb and flow of the generations of mankind lap up against Civilization and erode that which makes its name a living form versus a destiny of ruin. What can men do against such natural power amongst such feckless bureaucrats and laymen?

Tradition tells us we cannot command the tides as Canute the Great demonstrated, the natural forces pay no heed to our hubris, so we steel ourselves against it. Today we see "progress" advocating weakness, conformity, and cowardice as virtues. These are no longer sins, but constraints. For what is cowardice, weakness, and conformity but arbitrary interpretation? Nature's merciless bosom takes no prisoners. Prescience abandons us, but we can have faith in traditions because they are responsible for our existence. Denying traditionalism is spiritual suicide

It's difficult in contemporary society to define the purpose of traditionalism. Traditionalism carries weight, overbearing the confines of power. In one word we could define such as God. But that is meaningless to heathen brethren. It's like giving a map to the blind. We must dissect this term and put it into a concept that is materially chained to Man.

      Heathens know they are physical beings, temporal and sentient. Man has unearned knowledge, gained through his predecessors back unto the dawn of humanity. Such knowledge is now dispersed amongst many men, making up the corpus of all knowledge as far as man is concerned. If you took all of this knowledge and compressed it into a singularity, and incorporated all future knowledge, it would be omniscient, omnipotent, and omnipresent. What is the difference between this concept and "God"? Perhaps pride, hubris, or jealousy; in fewer words "sin". The Latin "sine" means "without" and so to be "in sin" is to be "without God", or in material terms: "to be without reference or remain ignorant of the corpus of human knowledge."

We cannot simply accept my definitions alone, so I have asked others for theirs. The first happens to be a recent mother, wife, and well-educated. She wished to remain anonymous otherwise:

"I don't know what traditionalism entails."

This is a common response from my experience. Hardly anything at all remains that might project and maintain the concept of traditionalism and so the majority of people are dumbstruck by the question. So entrancing is progress that tradition has become the pavement where progress trots, ignorantly wearing its cartwheels ever deeper into it.

This isn't the fault of any of these people, not you, me, and not my friend (who will likely read this), but occurred long before our births. We have LOST the basics of how to maintain and develop a strong society and culture.

God, even for heathens or atheists, can be based in material reality so their denial becomes irrational. This isn't a strawman. Faith is necessary because with unearned ancestral knowledge you cannot be certain. It's impossible to test without retarding development and material conditions. We must act out in faith to move forward. What is that besides traditionalism?

Another definition, this time by an excellent content creator named Aristocratic Utensil: *"A longstanding cultural bedrock that keeps society in harmony."*

It lines up with what has been laid out, and knowing Spoon is up to speed with problems in the West, it's accurate. I highly recommend checking out his Youtube Channel, which is both informative and fun.

He highlights issues like stability and harmony. I didn't prime anyone purposefully, so my point wouldn't be forced. We can see in Spoon's general definition the moving parts of traditionalism. Faith is blind, but you can attain insights through the study of history and theology.

Our listless leadership has replaced faith with a new priesthood and theology, with science and scientists to derive the truth. While this can certainly uncover "facts", it cannot itself determine what to do about them. You cannot derive an ought from an is (David Hume). There are no secular objective "oughts". All secular oughts are derived subjectively. One might claim that inherited wisdom is not objective because it relies on faith (in that it will work). The problem with such an argument is that it is self-evident that traditional structures function! So what they must argue is that we have faith in their "oughts" from "experts". To a mature and thinking man this is a further leap-of-faith than traditionalism informs! Our societal immaturity is unveiled.

Now for my long time online friend Michael and his view:

"When I think of traditionalism I think of people who want to return to a life prescribed by Christian family norms, but without the idea of obedience to God. They want the Protestant work ethic without the cross. They appreciate the values of the Christian society of their forefathers built, but they do not give glory to God. Instead, they credit "culture" or European heritage, or what have you. Although there are many traditionalists who rightly credit Christianity for the success and value of European traditional norms, in my experience they rarely credit the God of the Bible or Christ himself. This is their downfall."

This was a well-thought-out comment, coming from a decidedly Christian perspective. So is it true? I believe so. People often understand the wisdoms of the past but not necessarily why. As Micheal writes, many proponents of traditionalism wear religion as a skin suit upon the secularism just below the surface.

This is a lack of humility from a postmodern man. It's a sick perversion of traditionalism. Luckily we can still capture the hearts and minds of secularists and hopefully bring them back from the brink of spiritual disaster. There are no arguments remaining, only arrogance, hubris and incompetence! There is no argument between faith and logic, but instead we must reduce it to the difference between a trusted and relatively reliable faith principle and an unknown and completely blind faith which purports to be based on, quite literally, *measurement.*

Let's contemplate this for a moment. Let's say we have taken the local temperature, and behold it is 20°C! What men of the past would marvel and crouch down low at such revelation! With what reverence would they treat such astonishing datum! Of course, this is utter nonsense. There could be any number of ways in which this data could be interpreted. It's subjective. Yes the data itself, the measurement itself, is objective, this cannot be denied. But what one ought or ought not do about it, what direction this data must lead us towards, is subjective. What good is that in terms of "right" or "wrong"? They cannot be objectively determined by mere measure. They are subjective interpretations.

Secularism is not capable of guiding our actions rightly or wrongly, and so alone it's morally worthless! It's unprincipled, struggling to find meaning in the real world. Decisions become solitary moments in time, completely isolated from all precedence. You cannot carry a functional society forward from this basis, for all law is based on precedent! The Relative, secular idea is built upon sand and swamp. It is completely unstable. Only the fools and foolhardy build upon this precarious ground.

There is function in form itself, and if that form is solid then so will be its function. Forms which deny reality fail; there's a pressure pushing against it which cannot be withstood. Men are newborns in history. We are virtually blind at birth, and near-sighted from then on. Peering back in time we begin to transcend our myopia, if only slightly.

But by what means should one peer? History is unreliable and biased. One should consider at least two categories of quality. The first and most important is age, as the more ancient the knowledge the more it has been tried and tested, yet survived for us to read it. If after long epochs this knowledge is remembered, then it must be worth remembering. This becomes incredibly useful information, becoming embodied within man's being itself; it is not even uttered through straightforward language, but becomes part of a people. Society becomes incredibly rotten when this ethereal form is lost. People who question the value of such wisdom are as innocent and naïve as infants. The second aspect of quality is experience: "Has it worked?"

These narratives serve as magic potions to many ills, not by form but by function. When our stories speak of spells cast through magic ceremonies or rituals, they speak to a deeper meaning. It isn't that magic is being released outwards from a formless void, but that the immaterial wisdom is being grasped from what might appear as such but is actually the perpetuation of the immateriality of the past being pressed onwards. When you read old books today you don't imagine them as magic spells or formulæ, but as words. But that's what it's always been. It's deeply spiritual, the transference of past minds and being into yours, into your present, into your life, inevitably your future. There is no escaping this fundamental fact. We are the capacitors of culture.

People dismiss ancient wisdoms as outdated or inapplicable to their "unique" times. But this is wrong, and reveals a lagging creativity in such thinkers. Many ancient stories seem irrelevant today, but with some creativity we can renew them into relevance to derive a deeper meaning. They are tools as useful as their application entails. If you've never needed a screwdriver before, it was only useless to you until it was needed, revealing the temporality and serendipity of these things. More useful stories become our critical histories, the true survival necessities. But all stories, all ritual and tradition carry some higher purpose and meaning, even if that is simply to help remember the motions to act them out.

This is the truth from the mythos perspective. It is considered faith-based because it cannot be measured empirically, but experientially through acting out the wisdom in real life. Let's compare this to history.

History, or that which was written or recorded in the past, and perhaps reformed, recontextualized or rediscovered in the present, grants us limited insight into the human condition. One might think that the closer we are to the recorded events, the more accurate that interpretation will be; but the opposite is true. The nearer we are to historical events the less likely it will be true because we are blinded by interest and bias; we have too much to gain or lose personally.

The further we are removed from history, the less it will be affected by our bias and the errors we are prone to in reinterpretation. History may be useful, but ritual keeps it that way.

Narratives contain universal truths about the human condition without having to be tied to material reality like history requires. Take the example of Beauty and the Beast. There is a story on the surface that has characters going through a journey. But there is as much truth on the surface story as there is in each minuscule detail. For example, is there such a thing as a Beast? Yes and no. Every man has that potential, to be merciless, selfish and violent. But is that the only story being told? Is the story that Belle is simply a victim of some oppressive entity? Or is it the story of the heroic feminine, saving her father from her burden, to live under the custody of an unrefined, unreformed masculinity to relieve her father of the burden which is Belle? Is perhaps the withering rose not symbolic of a waning fertility, a limited window of time in which Belle must act in order to heroically perpetuate the despairing survival of humanity and civilization (at least in her corner of it)? Is it not true that by coming to accept her role as nature intended, to soften and subdue and accept the Beast, to turn him into a civilized being capable of love and care, to turn him, in a word, from a hedonistic heathen into a God-fearing Husband? Would the story be as interesting or compelling if it merely laid that out plainly without flourish or relevance to contemporary society? No, it must come whole-cloth. It cannot be deconstructed and remain the same form. It is key that we reimagine the story as time goes by, but the essential lessons must remain, the details too, or it will be lost, because it will otherwise be boring. Boredom is low level disgust, and disgusting things, even whole civilizations, are eventually tossed into the trash.

When we act out in faith to a "presented narrative", we become subject to its successes and failings. Unless the composer of such a narrative is unusually honest and perceptive, any composed narrative will not match reality as described. There are simply too many variables to account, so it will be wrong. It's not the fault of the author. The true failure on their part and on the part of all men is a lack of humility in assuming they perceive the world as it is versus how they want it to be. Our ancient stories are filled with warnings about humility. The phrase: "Fear of God is the beginning of wisdom." continually bears true in history. Even secularists will admit this.

The view of God as an embodiment of knowledge, as the culmination of all-there-is-to-know (as far as humans are concerned), is simply real. Physical beings exist only for one life upon this Earth, and if we spend the whole of it rehashing what has already been done, we stagnate. We must leverage the experiences of our ancestors in order to get ahead; in effect faith is the basis of civilization.

But let's complete the thought. Fear of "God" humbles oneself to unearned knowledge. For that which earned it is gone, long before us. This humility before the corpus of human knowledge is wisdom, which demonstrates respect for the persistence of reality and to recognize that our own narrative remains unfinished. This doesn't simply derail oneself from reality, but does so in a spectacular ball of fire from which there is likely no escape. Thus, the clear and opposite phrase can be determined as: "Pride cometh before the fall."

From secularity, what "God" commands means what previously earned human wisdom informs us on action. Its effectiveness being proven by eons of human survival, lest you become the exception to rewrite the book (which is always possible). Any tertiary understanding of mathematics and game theory will reveal to any reasonable person the truth that this is unlikely. Arrogance can overcome even the most sound of logic however, and so these types of people fall into a cycle of demise towards resentment. This appears with the power of a cyclone and whips up in destructive rage. Once petered out, it disappears, having destroyed itself. Its suicidal sentiments were unavoidable, the void being the problem from the start and it was pulled apart. Again we come up against a take on what it means to be "damned", to be "apart" from "God". In the secular interpretation this becomes clear. To be "apart from God" means to live in your own individualistic arrogance, to forsake the collective corpus of human knowledge in preference to one's own ego! From such much of the evil in the world flows out to drown the good and pure with selfish filth and depravity.

Man, today, and all men in their own times are seated as a minuscule speck of dust atop a massive stone pyramid of which we from its heights cannot see the bottom, which descends endlessly into the ephemeral mists of time. We can see some of what lay below us if we allow ourselves to look. By sheer happenstance we find ourselves on high, like all who preceded our ascent, here to be and to lay claim to our being. Progressives and Traditionalists alike marvel at our great height, but we differ in our thoughts on the above and below.

Progressives look at their place and look higher and beyond their present, while traditionalists marvel at what massive structure lay below, all of the past generations, their suffering, sacrifice, and struggle. In the minds of the traditionalists, without this underlying structure they would not be so-perched on-high, and instead we would be naked, cold, shivering starving prey; fearful of every snapping twig and rustling leaf...for who knows what creatures lurk amongst the shadows ready to pounce upon us and put our short miserable lives to an end?

Everything which is part of what lay below us protects us from such fate, such dire circumstances. We shall not gain good ground by looking at our own predecessors and making them enemies of perfection. We remove all preceding structures at our own peril; for we risk removing the very thing that has us so high; so doing would have us momentarily floating in mid-air like some cartoon. Perhaps that time has already come and gone, and now we observe the ground rushing up towards us at terminal velocity. Our arms flap wildly trying to cling to anything at all. Perhaps men and women have different natures? Nope, as this has been "deconstructed". Maybe the innocence of children should be maintained? CANCELLED! Perhaps we could vote ourselves back to normal? SORRY! This is now the new normal.

But what was the exact point of having gone "too far" with progress? Where was the system subverted? Well, it happened gradually at first, and then suddenly. Perhaps it was the swapping of masculine for feminine power? Any way you word it, it is not going to stop and it will only get worse before it can get better. I could be totally wrong. Perhaps we could foment a total revolution and clear everything out and reconstruct a better system that is an improvement from our state of decay and pozz; or maybe to do so risks a loss so immense that we cannot yet fathom it? Either way, the deluge cometh, so we must prepare.

"Hear you, O gallant, the sentry on the battlement?

Hear you what his song proclaimed?

We must now sunder, beloved man,

just as you only recently did hence depart,

when the day broke and the night,

like a fugitive, hastened away from us.

Alas, my dearest, I can no longer you veil.

The gloaming robs us of our joy.

O my rider, stand up, arise!"

(The Knight of Day, Otto bon Botenlauben, 1170 AD, Carmina Burana)

Much of the previous has to do with the importance of structural maintenance. Most people, if asked will be unwilling to trade what they have for something not guaranteed to bring an equivalent or improved return (those others we call gambling addicts).

The aversion to loss is greater in most cases than the willingness to risk existing assets. This alone should well-indicate the value people give to the preservation of known values, stability; this is a fundamentally conservative and traditional-based point-of-view.

The key to anyone's well-being is directly related to how ongoing their physical security and stability continues into the future. This security is always in reference to the known, also known as the past, and how the person can relate that past with the present. Does this coordinate well with the person so that they feel secure? It all depends on that structural maintenance referenced earlier.

With stability in such maintenance secured, it then must persist. This becomes a conflict of will versus entropy. It again is not just some simple task, and with it comes a whole new set of problems and solutions. Within the limited human lifespan it is key not to make too many avoidable errors, and so we build structures which persist to help in this. Enough compounded avoidable errors will crush a man's life to dust, never mind those errors which are completely unavoidable.

These structures are a map, not a despot, to advise on what has been previously successful and what failed. You can never expect a clear image or reference however, because the past is an ever-deepening abyss blinded by fog. But even through the abyssal fog a particular logic shines through: you have one known life upon this Earth as man, and so you must use your time wisely; every wasted moment is forever lost and can never be regained, and in a sense enters into the Bestial unconscious. The more time and energy someone wastes, the more someone spiritually becomes an animal, the more chaotic and disorganized they grow, the more predatory and dangerous (though in many forms) they become to others, especially the vulnerable. The Smashing Pumpkins' lyrics are correct: "The killer in me is the killer in you."

Even domesticated men are no angelic creatures, for many so-called domesticated men are killers, rapists, and otherwise negatively productive criminals. Many productive people even have these problems and lash out for seemingly no reason. It is in our deepest natures to be as such. Man is only domesticated as much as his needs are satiated, and this comes at the cost of maintaining our structures.

Work is how we maintain our civilizational infrastructures. Work has been severely atomized in our postmodern era. The vast majority of people are completely disconnected from the fruits of their labour, and even more kept distant from the products of their consumption. This fundamental disconnect enables the average person to question their conditions, which power cannot easily justify.

There certainly is a justification for material conditions (life being suffering), but there is little to justify their meagre share of the spoils. In reality there could be many reasons why to justify relative position within a system, but none that objectively matter, except in the cases of extreme specialization as per market mechanisms. Over time, even competency becomes nepotism and insider trading. Standards plummet. At first gradually, then later on quickly and suddenly. When this comes to a head the weakness is unveiled and the structure comes under threat by the rage-blinded "peasant" class, in a near-Marxian manner. This was the preferable scenario, but the ability of humans to endure suffering is quite astonishing. Many go their whole lives in a manner of complete and utter drudgery with no light at the end of the tunnel besides the belief in the afterlife. Perhaps such is just their natural instincts in postmodern form. Perhaps they have simply been conditioned into accepting their lot in life.

Many of our leaders in the West are completely incompetent. That our systems are so fragile should be an indication to many that something is wrong. But time and time again these weaknesses are masked through propaganda, and the anger and frustration is redirected to something else, something less critical. But for how long can that charade continue?

"*O Fortuna,*

variable in phase like the moon

always you wax or wane:

detestable is your life's way!

Now she palsies, then in sport she spurs

the acuity of the mind;

penury, power

she dissolved like ice."

(Stanza 1, O Fortuna, Carmina Burana)

It is like as a society we are heaping more and more onto a single pile, like an immobile scapegoat which we cannot drive into the wastes. The pile has grown so tall that we are shadowed more and more by it as things around us grow darker.

But I can see it! Its towering immensity does not relent! Like the permanent fixture of the Great Pyramid of Giza, like the Colossus of Rhodes when it stood, it beckons forth our inescapable ruin! No one that I know, or very nearly, could be forewarned. No one will know what to do anyways as they are so thoroughly drowned in this dark progressive miasma.

"Fate- monstrous

and empty,

you whirling wheel

you are malevolent,

well-being is vain,

and always fades to nothing,

shadowed

and veiled

you plague me too

now through the game

I bring my bare back

to your villainy."

(Stanza 2, O Fortuna, Carmina Burana)

We continue therefore on our journey towards folly. We forsake traditionalism and its warnings at our own peril. What lessons can we hope to gain through the immensity of our collapse? Why must men suffer such ruthless disregard for reality? Do we not deserve this? We scream from the highest hilltops for our fate as is, yet we do not know what incantations we shout! We beg for our damnation and lament not our hubris, but our prudence!

"Fate is against me,

in health

and virtue

driven on

and weighted down,

always enslaved.

So at this hour

without delay

pluck the vibrating strings;

since Fate

strikes down the string man,

everyone weep with me!"

(Stanza 3, O Fortuna, Carmina Burana)

The song I have been showcasing here is interesting because it comes from a time before the Renaissance and taps into traditional takes which today might fall upon deaf ears, insofar that they are not psychologized away. But this song along with many others, are not mere songs meant to numb our suffering minds and toiling bodies, they were sung as an acknowledgement of life and our suffering fate. They conveyed our limited lives in terms of both time and space, and to be grateful for and respectful of our own relationships with others. To appreciate the good while it lasts and to be prudent in our actions and decisions. This song "O Fortuna " for example highlights the suffering dismal life of someone as an example to all. Reader, go now to youtube and find a rendition of "O Fortuna" and listen to it in its original Latin. Even nearing a thousand years removed, the emotion and feeling is present, even to us ignorant and arrogant postmodernists. I doubt much contemporary music will be so affective towards our descendants a thousand years hence. I am not saying there is therefore no value in contemporary music, but simply that it is not *as* universal.

"I bemoan the wounds of Fortune

with weeping eyes,

for the gifts she made me

she perversely takes away.

It is written in truth,

that she has a fine head of hair,

but, when it comes to seizing an opportunity

she is bald.

On Fortune's throne

I used to sit raised up,

crowned with

the many-coloured flowers of prosperity;

though I may have flourished

happy and blessed

now I fall from the peak

deprived of Glory.

The Wheel of Fortune turns,

I go down, demeaned;

another is raised up;

far too high up

its the king at the summit-

let him fear ruin!

for under the axis is written,

Queen Hecuba"

(O Fortuna, Part 2 [I bemoan the wounds of Fortune], Carmina Burana)

Queen Hecuba was the Queen of Troy, mother of Hector, Paris, and Cassandra (amongst many others), as well as the wife of King Priam, as told in Homer's Iliad. According to legend she was wealthy beyond belief until her fall along with Troy, but (according to some legends) became enslaved by Odysseus, and then the Gods transformed her into a dog so she could escape. I say according to legend because we of course cannot absolutely confirm it, but yes the story is true in as much as it is narratively true (we'll conveniently ignore the dog transformation part), and the story is human. The narrative highlights fundamental truths of what it means to be human, and the cyclical natures of failure and success.

But what am I getting to with all this? What is the purpose for writing this short treatise on the traditional? I am trying to draw a line between good and evil, which runs through the heart of every person (Alexander Solzhenitsyn). Evil is a lack of prudence and forethought; it is destruction for destruction's sake, pain for the sake of pain. Both pain and destruction come for us and there is no escaping it. But let us not be plainly cruel or evil to ourselves and others simply because in the end we are all dead anyways. Such is not the philosophy of even barbarians, for they too more often than not carried a wide array of virtues based on fate. Instead such is the philosophy and *esprit-de-vie* of criminals, murderers, and other relativists.

To a relativist nothing is truly sacred, for nothing matters except for its relation to them. This is a dangerous type of person in any circumstance. There is little to value in current society because they see it as transitory as they see themselves. In fact from their point-of-view all is equally transitory. Nothing matters. Not their family's friends, and especially not their lovers, partners, husbands or wives; even their children are ultimately transitory to them.

None of their relationships are enduring, and even those which seem so, are often insincere and phoney. It leads many into depression with some finally seeking out a sense of community (having destroyed their natural one) and like an addict (which many are simultaneously) will latch onto anything which bumps their dopamine, no matter how shallow, and will pretend with this mode until it becomes time to run, and their transitory pattern continues. They will never settle, caught in some place between civilization and chaos: the untrammelled wilds to prey upon the weak and vulnerable as if to spread their illness like seeds into a compost heap at a Garden's edge.

These types come in many forms, and some are quite sophisticated, but be not swayed by their charms, they would kill if it aided them in their quest. If they don't rape, they will leave their children orphaned instead, for not even their own flesh and blood carries permanence. Like Dostoyevsky's Underground Man and his progressive ideology, his mind is captured and driven off a cliff along with all his passengers, and then abandoned in the midst of nonsense and chaos. If not for the stoic-stubbornness of traditionalists, it too would falter under the brow of transitory relativism, but it too is in shambles in comparison to what it once was. Perhaps a renewal could alter our fates? But how?

What the West in large part is suffering is a loss of trust and continuity in our communities. Our cultures have been eaten away from the inside, which veils the reality of our complex problem. Suddenly it has burst forth like a leopard from within, biting, clawing and scratching at our collectivity, ripping us apart. I have no solutions. I do have an unsurprising prediction however.

The renewal of the West will commence like the two major characters upon which we idealize its foundation. Like Socrates and Jesus Christ, we must first observe and experience fully the Crucifixion of Truth, so that the full and complete encounter with evil can steel us against this happening again for at least a little while. Problem is, between the crucifixion and the adoption by Emperor Constantine was nearly three centuries. Cyclically speaking that is the sort of temporal distance we are dealing with, at least with Rome. Can we close this gap more quickly?

There is only one other way for us to fix this problem (which is essentially what would be accomplished through crucifying the truth), but it would require the vast majority of people to realize what is happening by neglecting traditional values and wisdom. We possess the shortcuts to help ourselves if we would only take them seriously. In short we need to rediscover "God" to save ourselves. And as I have outlined earlier, even an atheist can believe, and they must if we are to succeed, for faith the size of a mustard seed can move mountains.

CHAPTER SIXTEEN:

Interregnum: The Indefinite nature of Democracy

There is a space of time that between two definitive points, called the indefinite. It is the difference between "the" and "a/an".

A nation could be any nation, while *the* nation is an identifiable entity. No one cares about a king, a president, a Prime Minister, a pope, or a bishop. They who care give reverence to the king, or whichever other leader they accept. The definitive, it is personal, actual; it is the synthesis of the de jure and the de facto. It is stable, a rock amongst the rapids in the river of time fasted to the bottom like an anchor, saving all who are graced by its steady presence from the swirling entropic torrents below.

Such definitives are times of plenty and order. Men can put down roots and build lives in its security and stability. These are the eras in which civilization is made or decline is stayed, temporarily. When in life we are definitive, we possess something immaterial with which we take ownership. Thus we struggle for it whatever the cost. This particularism, rather than the indefinite "universalism" is the foundation of civilized man, and thus civilization.

The diminution of the definite, of the particular and the personal, is the murder of the possessive spirit regarding mankind, and its psycho-spiritual constructs. This evidently leads to decline, for then all significant investment into the future halts as there is no longer certainty; only chaos and fear that the investments will be lost.

Short-term thinking results and short-life history strategy becomes the norm. An air of "après moi, le deluge" (after me, the flood) comes into fashion, and soon the prophecy comes true. During the French revolution, the deconstruction of the Ancien Régime led to a vain attempt to restore meaning to the new Republicans, who struggled, drowning in the hollowness of being, in parallel with the masses of their fellows who were actually drowned in the Loire by their zealous hands.

The events of the French revolution are not on our minds enough, and certainly not enough to avoid a repeat of its horrors. This should weigh upon us heavily but doesn't. This drive towards the indefinite was what ousted the particular King, for a republic so indefinite that it couldn't determine guilt by its own machinations and so nearly all accused were marched to the gallows or drowned. Women, children, the elderly: it mattered not; even infants were murdered (often by bayoneting.) In this instance in interregnum, the scum and villainy boiled to the top. Great evils were done because the good allowed it out of fear, cowardice, or whatever else drove them to inaction. This is banality, the letting things collapse, ironically foretold by the Sun King Louis XIV himself.

We in the west are in a period of interregnum. Law and order is retained like a stuck shadow. Our rulers see it for the weakness it is and so stack shadow upon shadow in order to strengthen it and improve resilience. But shadows cannot be strengthened, and in any case, the weakness in law is not a lack of law but a lack of leaders to wield it. Our leaders too are shadows, empty vessels, spiritless, fasted to their false gods they call progress and tolerance. They tolerate too much and discern too little; their morality is twisted. They sacrifice children's innocence and in many cases lives for material gain, or justify it with backward morals.

Consider as well, the complete cowardice shown during the Covid-19 pandemic. Many are far more guilty of cowardice than they would like to admit. It may have made logical sense at the start in some measure due to the fear of the unknown, the associated propaganda, and fear porn being beamed at us every minute. But even today "government officials" push an ineffective, dangerous experimental gene therapy to the masses, as if they don't know the ruse is up. Today we still see many wearing masks out in public and no one has the courage to criticize them. At this point, they should be mercilessly mocked and bullied like they meekly did to the free-breathers and pure-bloods in the midst of their isoflavonic panic! All of this was performed live on air by our political "leadership ". Your paper "rights", and your bodily autonomy, all surrendered like you were conquered. Because we are ruled by barbarians.

These are the fruits born through short-term thinking. We allow a façade to persist in promoting ideas of long-term planning, but it is fake. Everything is based on the panic-stricken now, financed through our futures, slowly beckoning the fate of civilization as if all is shrunk into the timeline of a single man's life. Nothing great could be conceived but a great consuming ruin.

No, we feast on false nutrition in the form of soyslop, leaving us fat, weak, and emotional. This lack of self-control creates a ceaseless cycle, like a snowball, rolling downhill and growing ever more rotund with each turning, like the turning of the earth, the girthy mass expands and becomes normalized. Day, night, day, night... and despite these constant cycles, these giants do not awaken. They perpetuate their soy-slumber, or embrace death in as cowardly a fashion as they can muster. A life lived as a life lost, sacrificed gleefully to the cause of gluttony. Even our diets are in interregnum. Nothing short of a complete overthrow of our false kings and stewards can change this. Anything outside of that will fail to halt this slide into absolute decline. As it stands, this decline is inevitable. Satiated, soy-sodden slobs slap their suppered stomachs as they slide their gargantuan ghastly guts into a glamourless abyss of bestial bliss. So consumed by vice, so is consumed the civilization which molded these monstrosities.

These intruding stewards who hammer us with their vile weapons, worship a number of false gods to which they are driven to subject you to. The first is equality which posits that all life should be fair because all people are equal and so all failures must be the fault of a system and not the failed individuals, who could be endlessly re-molded to suit the needs of the steward and power.

Man, according to them, is nothing but the will made flesh, and have the will incongruent with that of power he shall be bent to it. Such is believed by the authoritarians of all men, who see them as nothing but fleshy extensions of their will. The now common reliance of power on so-called "experts" for decision-making is little different from that of the past priestly classes reading the entrails of sacrificed animals to determine the actions leaders should take. By favoring equality as a prime value we see that competence's place on the planet has been usurped, and so in this illogical "rationality", decline ceaselessly proceeds.

The second god of their fancy is "diversity". This is power through the logic of division and destruction. Through this division, the steward rarely competes for the throne because no faction is large enough until some faction or other is able to ally with or conquer the others wherein it can be on a level playing field with Steward power. This division favors the Steward but weakens the security of the state. The Steward is an illegitimate ruler, of which he is aware. He is most concerned with his own power, a fact that cannot be ignored. As a result of the inward focus, outward focus diminishes, eventually weakening to the point where barbarians outside the walls cannot be kept at bay by force, for the force of the nation under the steward has turned too inward. Therefore, they are kept at bay by reputation or bribes. In some cases, these barbarians are integrated into the nation. This doesn't prevent but merely stalls the coming conflict. By various means, the steward drains the national coffers and then drains the people entirely.

This begins to fracture his alliances and a tyranny grows. In turn, this brings disparate groups together out of survival necessity, and so the already delicate social fabric, this steward's choice of Cultural Mosaic, cracks, and the underlying period of interregnum reveals itself. The society must choose either the particular definitive ruler, like the king, or rule by the indefinite, which may present itself in forms like a republic, democracy, or council of sorts. Thus we have this contrast between regnum and interregnum.

How do we know whether or not we are in Interregnum now? In interregnum, those in power seek to achieve legitimacy, having various methods. One is through putting to paper the limitations of both the "power" of power and the "rights"of the "people". But keep in mind that these paper rights are in constant flux. As time goes by power will tend to consolidate and expand itself, while restricting the rights of the people. Paper rights are essentially a document meant to gain the submission of the population in question. It is in many ways much worse than a serf contract, which is at least unbreakable at both ends. Before you laugh that away, serfs lived in relative equality with their lords, often out together at public houses and inns, and also attending the same religious sermons. Compared to today, the gap between a serf and his lord was minimal and in many ways was much more cooperative than we are taught today in our liberal paradigm. This was a major complaint from those on the political left, yet strangely, none now advocate for a return to serfdom. In any case, we will probably continue through many iterations of interregnum until our society reaches a cultural sink deep enough that the long-buried bones of a long-waiting king can be revealed and elevated to take his rightful place at the head of the nation.

Many view the rise and fall of the Roman republic as representing the majority of Rome's greatness. I contest here given my previous arguments that the Republicans represented instead interregnum. The last Roman king, Lucius Tarquinius Superbus came to power through the murder and assassination of his wife and elder brother. Is this not itself a decline in regal quality? It is certainly an indicator and was definitely used as justification for overthrowing the monarchy.

This new Roman republic went forward and expanded until it became swollen and corrupted, until a person of great courage in the right spot and at the right time, decided a change of course was necessary. First, we have the rise and fall of Julius Caesar, and the beginning of the Roman Empire, a return to the definitive.

It is already well understood that in post-empire Rome, during the rule of Odoacer, as king of Italy, a feudal or monarchical system persisted up until (at least in name) the Italian republic was done away with in 1946! Certainly, there were a number of different kingdoms, city-states, and minor principalities within what has become contemporary Italy, but such a particular definitive form in one way or another lasted some 1453 years! This is of course a longer length of time than Constantine's city: Nova Roma (Byzantium/Constantinople) lasted under "Roman" rule (from 330 A.D. to 1453, A.D, approximately 1123 years). Keep in mind that Byzantium itself was under a definitive model of governance.

Consider as well that prior to the advance of "democracy", most military conflicts involved only hundreds to perhaps thousands of soldiers, essentially exclusive to the upper-class elites and handfuls of retainers or conscripts. But after the French revolution and the *Levée en Masse*, any army that didn't include the whole national effort for total war, was doomed to fail, and so democracy ever since has become a government of total war and violence unlike anything seen before, outside some of the classical civilization and the Far East.

I am here to establish a new point of view, that despite the pomp and ceremony, despite the semblance of law and order, and despite our own alleged rights claims, we are in a time of interregnum. When did it begin? It will vary by place; for instance, for the French, it would have been during the French revolution; for the Russians during the Bolshevik revolution. From here, things get controversial. The ending of the British empire, it would likely be for the Brits; and most likely in the founding of the USA for

Americans. The end of World War I it was for the Germans. 1944 for the Icelanders. 1889 for Brazil. Included in the ending of the British empire is the tragic case of Canada formed in 1867 to be smothered in its own crib; this was formalized in 1982 with the Canadian charter of rights and freedoms, which is a magical piece of paper capable of containing all of Canada's hopes and dreams so that they can be crumpled up and tossed away by the courts.

However, which way you think of it, damning evidence breaks the liberal delusion of functional and stable democracy. There never has been one, and our largest wars, which killed more people than under any other system, have always been under the auspices of indefinite systems like democracies and republics. Indefinitive government is met with unending indefinite problems, and these problems will continue until a definitive solution beckons forth from the chaos or ruins, and makes right which has for so long been wrong. Long live whosoever King that be.

CHAPTER SEVENTEEN:

Precipice: Authoring Caesar Part One

Western man stands on a precipice before a path ridden with obstacles; behind us lay our progenitors: "old", "obsolete", and "incapable". Whiffs of their essence lay within us, hopefully enough to make a difference. Ahead lies our future, our progeny, and all we will, our canvas. We cannot correct the sleeping, dead past; the horns at the battle of Jericho could not wake it. We must do the needful. This grows more obvious each day that we seek out righteous justice, our birthright. We need the embodiment of our idea in human form, a Caesar, a leader who must come before the decline, lest civilization slide in retreat. We must overlay and superimpose our treatise on being; the man who halts the fall, we must author our truth, and with it weave our Caesar and by his will, the World.

But how fasted to the rotted moulding canvas of the so-called "enlightenment" have we become? What past stories were corrupted and stained, even unwittingly, by enlightenment impressions? What if this is a useless fantasy bordering on the schizophrenic, and what could providence imbue within us? Have we not been blinded by this malfeasance? How long have we drifted without a helm or keel? How long since we torched our sails and fanned the flames with our prods and paddles? Our civilization huddles in the damp dark recess, staring into the abyssal deep, pleading for mercy. Kali Yuga yawns.

In our Plato's cave, we stare at the shadows on the walls and destroy the insane who deny our reality. No man directly accesses another's mind except through stories. These stories become our reality through reference and relation! Through it men are directed to whichever action narrative power demands. Mercy only comes when the authors command it. How much of what we "think" comes from what we experience? How can we conceive of experience without reference? And what of ourselves can we reference? Virtually nothing! Nearly all our reference comes from without, not within. The world-historical epoch (regardless of who or what has written it) is larger than us. We are at its mercy (and believe me, it will show us none); and so we see only what we are shown.

There is a gulf between seeing and being shown. A wild mountain goat sees the world, the dangers, and predators; he is free to live and die by his own bloodied struggle; a sheep is penned, curated and mastered over to live and die at the hands of their shepherd. They see the shepherd's world as their existence. The Pasture. The Crook. The Shepherd. Sheep never see the knife that takes its life, and only realize it's over when it's too late.

Curation vs. Instinct

Curation, "advertisement", "education", scopes and forms. All undeniably push out a vision of the world to show you, not merely what to see but how. Selection of particular commentators, or to have commentators at all! Editorial control, selection of viewpoints; each contributes to power over a narrow range of permissible perspectives, allowable outcomes, and particular narratives. This authors and authorizes a narrow bandwidth of what "reality" is, and which reality you must own and avow; and you must profess this "reality". To question or deny it is "demented" despite it meaning that one's mind has become lost, "de-minded", to think outside the "permissible bandwidth", despite the contradiction in terms. Although there are plenty of demented people who are quite outside the bandwidth, there is a difference between an insane (and pasteurized) sheep and a wild mountain goat.

This curation becomes like a dam on a river, rarely releasing powerful torrents downstream. Over time it curates more elaborate lies, building the dam higher and broader. The waters build up behind it, flooding more and more of the rear terrain, with more people abandoning the area (as alone the narrative structures cannot support the conceptual load). The amassing waters become undeniable over time, and soon the dam is so high it cannot support the rise. Though the dam may from time to time release some waters, extending its power over time but with diminishing narrative momentum, eventually the dam cannot withstand the weight, the deluge washes forth, wiping away the narrative curation that once blinded all, the truth is set forward and the whole thing collapses. But what is this dam of our "narrative reality" which holds us back from solving the moulding rot with which we currently suffer?

In the enlightenment view, history is progressing along a linear path, always improving upon the material human condition (and in some views the immaterial). It imagines that the human condition will continually improve, reaching or exceeding a state of civilization similar to Gene Roddenberry's "Star Trek", where man goes without the struggle for material wealth, living in Utopic plenty. One would imagine that this would lead to a lack of conflict, for what need would conflict serve under even a relative utopia?

But even Star Trek cannot imagine this. Conflicts exist in this narrative where humans compete, work with, destroy, and are destroyed by varying alien species. Why? Well even Star Trek isn't "Utopic". It is rife with material and immaterial conflict over resources, influence, and control. This is fundamental to reality because limited resources bring competition. In contrast, demand is ceaseless, limitless, except for the dead.

If you meet the needs of a population, they will grow, and then need to expand resources or the new population will go without. This creates expansion pressure. If you create a system that controls population growth, you instead have pressure against natural human behaviour, a pressure of its own, leading to competition within that system, creating conflict over internal control and power, or overprivileged access to the limited resources within the limiting system. The continuous progress of the human condition is not linear, but cyclical, and even if one denies the proof of history, it is proven through the logic of growth maximization leading to shortage and decline when a group fails to expand their resources. It is proof through pain.

Wisdom vs. Knowledge

Wisdom and experience will always trump knowledge and theory. Wisdom comes from the experience of real-world conditions, as it has contended with and overcome unforeseen conditions and circumstances rather than mere human imagination. Good evidence for this has been pouring out of journals and academic papers regarding the decline in rates of innovation since 1873 AD. During the First and Second World Wars, there were still many innovations per capita, though even by then it had dropped significantly. That drop however is nothing like what we are seeing today: we are reaching levels of innovation nearing that of 1455 AD.

This decline is happening despite the centralization and systemization of corporate bodies having access to a much broader swath of the population but also a greater ability to bring these particular and rare people together to combine their talents. Despite this as well, innovation is dropping off a statistical cliff. We do not know yet what the cause is, but one might speculate that the lack of liberty when it comes to innovation, combined with the lack of urgent necessity (perhaps as a result of decadence), and then looking at the managerial incentives demanding "something to show for the investment of time and money" leading to middling, stagnant, and inconsequential changes, combined again with a homogeneous monolithic corporate culture, one might possess a modicum of theory as to how we got here.

Throughout the 20th Century, the size of the State, Corporations, and Unions grew massively, and innovation declined similarly. For as much as the existing power structures want to signal diversity, inclusion, and equity, we find our systems becoming more and more uniform, exclusive, and unfair.

The theory of linear history holds little weight in comparison to the obvious, clear, and experiential existence of cyclical history. For all the talk of linearity, we see no progress within the framework. If linearity were true, "progress" should occur when theories posited through it are practiced, leading to incremental change.

With welfare, for example, the idea is that recipients would get a hand up from a bad situation, so they didn't have to suffer, and get their life together to get employed or start a business. Instead, welfare has bred generations of people who rely on the dole, who spend their whole lives contributing little to nothing to the greater society. In many cases, they not only take through the dole systems (welfare/false-claimed disability) but they actively damage the system (theft, rape/violence, murder). They become dependent on the dole, which is by any normal measure, regression.

Poverty too runs cyclically, or perhaps it appears linear but soon devolves into a death spiral of maximized suffering. Very rarely does someone escape welfare traps, but the system makes these success stories the narrative focal point. Each and every time a proponent of the linear view is shown a failure in their theory, they explain it away as if it wasn't the fault of theory, but of practice. It is utterly contemptible and cowardly.

Democracy vs. Power

Western "democratic institutions" (as they would self-describe) are a tremendous cope for the boomer generation which has utterly failed to understand their world-historical place. This system of interlocking institutions once offered the greatest material wealth in not just the contemporary world, but all of world history! Now, as it fails to provide basics like decent food and housing to an ever-shrinking middle-class, the eternal Boomer clings to their "constitution", "charter", and "patriotism", like the pathetic character of Uncle Rico from the film Napoleon Dynamite, reminiscing:

"...Yeah... Coach woulda put me in fourth quarter, we would've been state champions. No doubt. No doubt in my mind."

But the fourth quarter came, Boomers. The fourth quarter came and the coach (fate) put you in at QB. You made one throw for a few yards, things were looking okay. But then you did a QB sneak and got hammered by the linebackers. All you have done for the forty years since is take a knee and run out the clock. The now common kneeling at sports games is the ultimate Boomer surrender. You think you won, but you were already losing. You were coaxed by the media and authors of your reality to blow through your children's inheritances in the biggest YOLO in human history. You grew lazy, fat, and degenerate. You stopped building and never stopped consuming.

Yet Boomers (and others) still cling to the notion of democracy, as if it were some sort of god. According to H.H. Hoppe, this god failed, and Boomers who cling to hope are floating on a stinking, rotting corpse. Likewise, Boomers are created in the image of their failed god and are taking on the same stinking, rotting form. Now having melded with the object of their worship, cannot separate in any meaningful manner. The Boomers cannot save us. The Boomers can't do anything at all, especially at this point. They are political zombies:

"Consume low-quality boomer memes. Self aggrandize. Do nothing. Do not even respect the world in flames enough to piss on it. After all: Après vous, le déluge."

The solution must come from the millennial generation. Yes, that's a stark realization, I know. But the Zoomer generation is incapable. Generation Alpha is hardly out of diapers. Generation

X has no more possibility than the Boomers do because they are essentially nihilists. It will be the millennials who stand to inherit most of the problems directly. Millennials cannot afford homes. This is a historical failure beyond the magnitude of most problems, given it is such a simple issue to deal with in any other time. The combination of the insane Boomer drive to have the home serve as a savings and retirement account, along with the insane Boomer drive to preserve the value of that investment through strict zoning and housing by-laws, by which they benefit directly at the expense of everyone else in the market through control of effective housing supply.

People who say: "We need regulations or things will become chaotic" never look at the actual consequences of their position, being that their children and grandchildren will never own a home, if they even have offspring or heirs, and so our civilization will eventually disappear. When they later come to claim: "We didn't know any better," well they are damn right! And if you don't know any better then you don't start tearing down fence posts whose purpose you don't understand.

This idea is lost on them. They will not get it nor will they ever agree. But this doesn't matter as it is only a stumbling block if you think democracy has value. What needs to be done, needs to be done. You cannot put all the economic power into a single class of people and have any sort of an honest system, because those on the outside will become either resentful and angry, or suicidally content. No civilization can survive this. So-called "Democratic norms" must be upended if any of our civilization is to survive. This is the only path, there is no time for any other route. Power must be taken and change must come or it will be curtains. To worship democracy now is to pray to a dead and false god. It is a suicidal death cult that needs to end. It needs to be cleared out. There needs to be a new start. This is an invocation of the cyclical historical view. The narrative is set, and one will rise to meet the challenge. Who will it be? Who will save the West from utter annihilation?

Will & Action

It is no longer a question of where "passive evolution" will take us as a civilization: destruction, the Great Darkness. To simply allow things to go on in some sort of passivity is to allow malfeasance to write our story, to make us the antagonist in our own narrative epoch. What scandal would that be? Hoisted by our own petard for all of human history? The civilization which at its peak, decided to starve itself to death because it could not sacrifice the Lamb for its own nourishment, ironically a symbol of Christendom and pre-Christendom for some twenty centuries!

The West needs someone with the will to act, the will to make sacrifice, the will to move the ball forward and push the rotting stink out to the heap of festering sewage to which it rightfully belongs. These institutions are rotten skeletal forms, ready to be the whip-hand for any worthy Caesar. The worst you can face is eternal, glorious death, and that certainly beats eternal insignificance. The struggle itself is inevitably gruesome: but the essential contrast is civilizational annihilation or glory beyond belief. If you cannot manage Caesarism, you must help author him into the world. Write about what must be done! Tell others what must be done! An Age of Heroes is inevitable, but it must be authored. You must give it the authority which it deserves. For every Iliad an Achilles, for every Achilles, an Alexander and, for every Alexander, a Caesar.

We must manifest the Great Man to awaken us from our decadent slumber. Every time the Boomer approaches the Rubicon he kneels and surrenders to the zombified God "Democracy" which progressives wear as a rotted-out skin suit. There is no God in that form to fear! The curtain is pulled back and you can see who wields the false forms behind! The disgusting flesh monstrosity makes the Boomer cower in fear, it is up to us to clear out the stinking filth and renew! Your right to rule is determined by the totality of your victory! Clear out the rotting filth!

CHAPTER EIGHTEEN:

Reaction: Authoring Caesar Part Two

The imposition of mob rule, the ultimate and end result of democracy, damages individual autonomy. It threatens and often eliminates your natural rights: life, limb, and property. We are at whatever mercy the mob grants us, if any. Every time a legislative body meets, all people are on the butcher's block, and all we can do is pray it's not us.

Our political power and political effect is completely irrelevant and moot. Our votes amongst the masses provides no security, no authority, no viable alternative to the will of the mob. Even worse, our vote signals our submission to the mob's will, granting them moral authority for whatever actions they press upon us.

As time passes in a democracy, more and more of our natural rights are surrendered as the degenerative forces of entropy erode the moral backbones of the defenders of our liberties. In substitute, our mobs emboss shiny papers with seals of "guarantees" which they grant us, stamped and signed by people long dead and buried, spinning in their graves.

In a mob you cannot own yourself, and all you create is at its mercy and whim. If you are lucky, the mob will ignore you. At some point however, the mob will turn and villainize you, and make a caricature of you. They can destroy you, everyone you love, and all you hold dear; by declaring you evil, or having gained through ill, by their sweat and blood. This won't be true and never need be, but those facts are immaterial to their case. In their resentment and envy there can be no mercies, nor Justice; for they are the Mob, and resistance is futile.

Democracy, especially in its current welfare-state form, likes to pretend it's superior to its "developing-world" counterparts with little warlords extracting fees to allow commerce and transit within its "territory", but there is little difference. It is simply veiled and hidden behind the taxes which cannibalize the most productive people, while also seeking out and destroying any chance to escape the grasping talons of the tax man. Though many do escape the oppression: the suffocating, relentless, oxygen-starved and brain damaged mobsters. They who are driven by envy and greed, project such a charge upon productive people, to justify their actions. This resentment and evil, can only be plied by an equivalent volume of intoxicants and sloth, granting the working people respite from the ever-present parasite.

For the mob, your private property and life are not yours. And the so-called defenders of your rights slowly but surely surrender yours to this mob if only to temporarily extend their political power. Over time these continuous slow surrenders and retreats accumulate within the bureaucratic framework and system, until oppressive policy changes drown away all economic opportunity, where finally the wellspring from which the whole progressive project runs dry, often followed by a great exodus, spreading the underlying resentment into the world. Though one might imagine that some introspection may be at hand here, it will not happen, and like a gangrenous infection, envy devours all.

One should not trust these same fickle structures which once openly and proudly murdered some of our greatest thinkers and spiritual leaders. It took a direct democracy to murder the Great Socrates, and a jury to both condemn and then fail to pardon Jesus Christ who died on the cross. Krishna in the Bhagavad Gita warns Prince Arjuna against these demoniac people and ideas. To them, he says, all truth is relative; all goals aim towards the maximization of material pleasures, without regard to expense to himself, others, or society in general. They are trapped in a sort of hell of consumption, while it consumes them. Their time is only considered in this regard, and so they waste much of it through sloth and inebriation.

Their life in-between pleasures is experienced as pure pain, to which they will pay any price to end, their wealth, their love, their souls. Forever they live in the present, rarely a thought is given to the future. They would burn down their home in the middle of winter to feel the increased warmth, soon to be left totally exposed and doomed. One would think they would do civilization a favour and just die, but they do not, and instead will burn their neighbours house to feel more warmth. This is how things regress away from civilized life and into brutal barbarism. Soon too, as this destructive psychic-prion exhibits its ruinous effect on the civilized, attacking humanity itself in an entropic spiral towards the bestial unconscious.

Once the decline begins, great poverty ensues. As the base structures dissolve due to the destruction, ill-maintenance, and buy-in incentive, an infrastructure shortage burgeons forth. Lesser, lower levels of infrastructure start to be used, which is less efficient, slower, and more expensive. In response, the prices of goods and services start to rise relative to the infrastructure efficiency loss.

At some point, more invasive and destructive methods of resource harvesting will ensue as the survivors of the interregnum/anarchy scrounge whatever they can however they can for survival. Groups will form, to mutually defend, maintain, and harvest resources and territories; and so a new feudalism forms over time. This feudalism will eventually result in a return to the natural and most stable human political system, Monarchy, through the ascension of a strong man, a "King". This king will not necessarily need to force his way into power, as the people will bring him forth as their champion of civilization.

As you can see, Caesarism is inevitable with Democracy.

Either the Caesar will come now and prevent the downwards slide, or arise once we have bounced up from rock bottom. There is nothing to lose through the ascension of a coming Great Man, and our whole civilizational infrastructure to salvage. We can always start from zero like we have many times, but we don't need to. It's through this cycle of low-born resentment in which humanity is destroyed. It can only be overcome through the will to power of a heroic Great Man. Rise, Caesar.

CHAPTER NINETEEN:

Emergence: Authoring Caesar Part Three

The greatest failure of Democracy is in empowering the incapable and immoral. This brings these wretches into an unfair conflict with moral and just people over power. Armed with this evil, the immoral wretches slash at righteous good, before good knows what hit it. Democracy breeds naïveté towards the human condition, leaving these good and upstanding people vulnerable; easy victims for those devoid of conscience and virtue; those who always seek out material wealth no matter the cost.

But how do you identify such wretches of society? Firstly by vice alone; not that any man is vice-free, he should at least aim towards virtue (to err is human), and not be drowning in vice. For if he is, he has fallen to the insatiability of material pleasure. This is a bottomless abyss which cannot be filled; a hole in the heart which swallows up girthy portions of dopamine-releasing debauchery, always leaving the degenerate madman in search of his next exposure. These power dynamics are antithetical to civilization. This is like having a nation run by drug addicts. How would that fare? In the past, degenerates didn't exercise their de jure political power, even with communists and socialists pleading with them and recruiting them: degenerates simply did not care.

Today, degenerates realize that they can use political power to fund ever more degeneracy than before, and so these parasites drink deeply on the civilizational lifeblood. They grow more numerous each day and will not stop. They drink until there is no more, and having been so bound to the host, will wither and die along-with. In the end, these degenerates are dead; any alternative proposition, so long as it results in their survival (assuming a desire to reduce or avoid death) is preferable to degenerates having power. Outside of the degenerate urge to destroy, nothing is gained by handing them power. Billions of lives hang in the balance.

Much of the developing world relies heavily on the high productivity of the industrial power farms in the developed world, without which starvation on unimaginable scales would sweep across the planet, resulting in untold chaos and an unfathomable loss of life. It would be immoral to allow so many such a horrid fate for the cause of rampant vice. If one has a heart and soul within them, one must do whatever one can to prevent this disaster.

So how do you know if you are right to act? What can you draw upon to willfully move with purpose? If you fail to figure out a way, you will soon be standing in the ashes of a billion souls and asking their ghosts what being entails. It depends on your values. When Balian of Ibelin asked what Jerusalem was worth, Saladin replied: "Nothing…Everything." (line from the film Kingdom of Heaven). Jerusalem itself was not any sort of strategic location, and held little material value. However the immaterial value of the city, the spiritual value, was priceless. Why? Objective measure cannot discern this, yet objective, secular science lays claim to revelation and truth. Still the account is immeasurable, unquantifiable, lost to science.

This is the reality in which we live, and the power of Jerusalem is in its narrative space. It is a civilizational reference point, a real physical place, and cannot be copied or reproduced. It is authentic so long as the narrative persists, and like a candle in the wind, mankind trundles forth with its Jerusalems in hand, navigating the darkness; the lonely lights pressing forth through aged and cracking hands, while demons hiss and spit at the flame, trying as they can to beckon a shadowy gloom. Should one be passive towards such demons? No! "Rage, rage against the dying of the light." -*Dylan Thomas*

We, the capable, must be strident, vociferous in our goals! We mustn't allow for the drowning shadows to eliminate our progeny! Passivity is our death by suicide! Jarring though it is for our spineless, faint-hearted postmodern types to suddenly hear, we must judge accurately and violently throw aside our rose-tinted glasses! The enemy feigns strength and sings loudly, but it's a farce driven by vice alone; they sound like they sing for power but cry out for release from their suffering in chains. Their sounds scream through their mortal coils and beckon forth the good and noble for righteous Justice! If you wish to be Christ-Like then start doing his work and face these prisoners of material degeneration.

We elect our leaders at every turn, and each vote is a secular prayer for absolution; in return we are rebuked and punished for our naïve weakness and frailty in failing to solve our own problems. We cannot blame the politicians, we the electorate are to blame for we too are incapable. We no longer choose leaders based on their virtues, but our vices. We damn ourselves from the start with weak and faithless hearts. Before we can hope to clear our the immoral democratic system, we must clear out the democracy within ourselves.

That being said, any human body run by a committee (like a democracy) would be in much the same state, close to death. It will take the will of the mind to repair the degenerate chaos, to make whole body and nation. A Monarch, a human head of state as the face of the country is preferable and more ideal than this mob-rule "democracy". Even if we consider that both a mob and monarch can be corrupt, evil, immoral, or unjust, it is far simpler to right a wrong King, than an unruly, incorrigible mob. But lo! Must the King be imbued with moral knowledge and know he can be held to account by a higher power? Yes, and a mob can never be. It is a necessary part of power for it to not create itself as a simulacrum of God. Woe to those who have faith in mobs, for it is a short and brutal life in the worship of materialism, whilst a King is never wanting for he owns all, thus his nation is a reflection of him, while the mob is an indignant abyss.

Even the filtered and curated history which we are permitted to view shows a cycle from mob to Monarch, wherein the nation gains wealth and power, to the point where the mob gets uppity and deposes the Monarch. This kills real prosperity and so this mob surfs the corpses of their ancestors to ruin. Arriving there they discover themselves in a materialistic hell, and eventually one great man comes to rise into power and in this apocalypse they become King. True this man is King of the Ashes but a King nonetheless, and from his direction and drive things improve. This drive from below, a King of Ashes and then the King of Marble, is essentially possible because the King possesses the moral and ethical strength to do so. Where Kings fail in history, they fail because they act immorally and do not think about the greater national project. They succumb to the mob-desires, the animalistic, anti-civilizational forces which the mob cannot repel; only man can, even though a man is weak and pathetic, lowly, wretched, irreverent; despite this it is the only way forward for advancing civilization. There is a reason why people used to pray for Queens and Kings.

It is not in our nature to reject temptation. We are evolved or have an instinct for gluttony (ceteris paribus). The more accessible we make the objects of our desires, the more we must possess the will to reject excess and needless waste. Not because we don't want it, but because it weakens us, it ruins us; whether by our own hands or from outside. The psychology of the mob is not one to reject plenty, it's not one to self-moderate, and so will nearly always give-in to excess.

The unwillingness of the mob to sacrifice for the greater whole, is evident. Even when one mobbite democrat sacrifices (as rare as that may be), it is done to signal complicity and virtue towards the mob, with a genuine self sacrifice being rather absent. It is simply not performed if the performance is unseen, and as society descends further, it will be performed less and less, soon not at all. In contrast a King can say no, a King can say enough is enough and end whatever nonsense is present once and for all.

The capacity for a King to say enough, whilst a mob is incapable, establishes the two as eternal rivals. This is however mostly one-sided with the King eventually being run-off by the mob, to begin the descent, and then the King arising once again to rebuild and bringing civilization back into ascension. This, the historical narrative within a cyclical vision of history, establishes the Mob as the narrative antagonist, with the King playing the protagonist who rebuilds from the ashes.

This of course assumes that the cause of civilization is positive in our view. I admit this is not everyone's view, but for the most part it is mine. With that, the linear or Whig view of history is clearly wrong. Things do not, and never have always been better. Things wax and wane with the ebbing and flowing of will and desire. For that to change we would need to change human nature, which is a failed enterprise.

But if descent and collapse is inevitable, due to the deposition of the King, could the collapse be halted with a Herculean effort of will through the enthronement of a talented Monarch, thus avoiding the stages of collapse such as the loss of knowledge and custom, the swimming in the ashes from which a King would arise anyways? Could we avoid the inevitable by thwarting the slide mid-way? Perhaps we can. Perhaps that's impossible. But whence has it been tried before? Could it be a civilizational shortcut? Or short circuit? God only knows.

CHAPTER TWENTY:

Faith and Believing: Authoring Caesar Part Four

"Where there's a will, there's a way:" all can be overcome through the power of will; but one must first possess it. It's been a long period of growth towards higher Civilization in the West. We have been seated high for so long that the notion of a precipice is foreign. Sliding downwards we accelerate, subtly, then suddenly. It is arguable as to when and where this downtrend began, and varies as much as the people you ask. Some say it was the fall of the USSR which caused complacency in the West. But the USSR was in collapse since its founding, in a struggle of its own in parallel with the West. But the USSR was less resilient and less capable of handling the entropic strain.

A Brief Exploration and Turn

Some say it was the Vietnam war, but that was a symptom. Some claim it was the second or first world war; the Treaty of Versailles; the Russian Revolution; the Russo-Japanese war; the Spanish-American war. No. These are symptoms of a grand malaise. What about the Napoleonic Wars or the French Revolution? The former a symptom; the latter a hatching egg.

Instead, I claim that the end of the upward struggle of the West is best defined by something seemingly unrelated: the first public performance of Johann Strauss II's *"Blue Danube"* which first played at Vienna's Diana Baths on February 15th 1867. It was also played at the World Fair in Paris that same year. In Great Britain The Fenian rising breaks out, beginning the end of British rule in Ireland. We also have the Luxembourg Crisis which nearly set off a Franco-Prussian war early (later happening in 1870).

Canada becomes mostly independent from the Empire in the same year; Alaska is purchased by the USA for $0.02 per acre from the Russian Empire, both of which come to undermine European colonialism. Alfred Nobel patents dynamite. The Emperor of Mexico is executed, and that same day Buenos Aires plays its first football match. Disraeli's Second Reform Act enfranchised nearly double the previous number of voting men as before. Karl Marx publishes his first volume of Das Kapital. This was also the last year penal ships were sent overseas from Britain. The Paraguayan War rages still in South America.

Asleep at the Wheel

Queen Victoria lost her husband Albert six years prior and remained in mourning the rest of her life, (outside of her Royal duties) essentially spending the remainder of her reign on vacation as a head of state in de facto absentia. The contemporary propaganda at the time conveyed a message of a massively huge and flourishing British Empire, when in reality in under a century, near wholly gone and nominally persisting as the Commonwealth.

Her Royal Highness, Queen Victoria, asleep at the Imperial Helm, died in 1901, crashing the British Empire onto the rocky beaches of the Isle of Wight, having long abandoned the necessary Imperial spirit. What would she have said had she witnessed the coming world war between her Grandsons, who sent millions of good and honest men to their deaths, instead spending some four decades moping around doing her Widow's walkabout?

For her reign, the Empire remained well-stocked with strong institutional momentum and so the necessary functions of the Empire carried on. By most recollections of history so far published, it was the glory of the Victorian Era! The great wonder of the Industrial Revolution! New Worlds! New Peoples! Technologies! Prometheus born again arises this new coal-powered prosperity and human development! The relevant statistics do not lie, though I will not bore the reader with them nor challenge them. But yes we have here in 1867 the peak of the British Empire. It wasn't clean-cut growth devoid of bloodshed, but in comparison to past empires it was one of the best to most people.

But not people like those who mine for coal; they who choke, cough, and perish, generation after generation in unimaginable poverty and privation. This sacrifice is surely considered while the British political elite invite half of the old empire to its shores. Even at the sacrifice of the progeny of the founders who toiled in the mines and fields, breaking both sweat and back for the good of the nation. Not a dozen years had passed from the death of Queen Victoria when these working men would be sent off to die in 1914 and onwards against the dreaded Kaiserreich in France, with millions slaughtering other millions in a pointless and stupid conflict that was entirely avoidable had better men been at the helm. These men today are all but forgotten, but for a poppy.

An Ode to Sacrifice: A Reflection

Today, thousands upon thousands of foreign hordes land upon British beaches, looking for a handout, claiming to be refugees. Should the good Brits rise up to repel the invader, the State will smack you down, attack you, and punish you over your transgressions, treating you as an insurgent against the Crown. Who voted for this? No Brit did, yet in lockstep all parties impose it on the British people. This policy has nothing to do with democratic will, so what causes this? Perhaps the government can do nothing about it, the UK despite its pomp and ceremony, is in a period of chaotic interregnum. With a limited state apparatus, it chooses to expend resources on foreign interests at the expense of domestic interest; this is completely unique in history. One might think this is a function of basic governance, but given the total inaction, given it is a popular issue (stopping the crossings) perhaps the whole of the UK government is a façade, an imperceptible spirit, a ghost government propped up by a great game of mass media charades!

Surfing the Kali Yuga

Consider the NHS. Has it ever been worse? What about the preservation of historical monuments and places of history concerning English and British heritage? Priceless castles and artefacts, strewn about the countryside with little to no maintenance , falling apart, to ruin, kept barely there by the fledgling English Heritage society begging for donations? Why?

The UK, which is not alone in the world, a corporate zombie-state with only the basest central nervous system, each limb operating independently from the main body, in a constant war of attrition and slowly tearing itself limb from limb, only to stitch parts back on haphazardly, creating enormous festering scars and wounds, with indigenous Brits running for the hills and the yonder shires to escape the chaotic malaise of the major metropoli.

Where are we now?

We are very much today in a similar circumstance to 1901. The Queen has died. She was held in great reverence. Her son, at this time an old man, has ascended to the throne. He has no cousins seated throughout the thrones of continental Europe, yet still we are on the verge of world war. Escalation is in the cards, the great central alliance readies itself. The EU stands alongside its Imperial Suzerain NATO, in defiance of the Russian intervention in the Donbas region of what was Ukraine. Nuclear threat keeps a world war at bay, but for how long?

How many Russian men can be destroyed by western supplied arms before Russia and Putin are provoked to total war escalation? What will NATO do should Russia be taken from the board? Will the thoughtful, wise, but formerly *oppressed* Russian people now elegantly kneel towards the purely moral and ethical propositions of Global Homogeneity? Perhaps Russia too, is in an interregnum? Should Russia lose Putin, what good can that do for the West?

Any? It would create a power vacuum worse than in the former USSR in the 1990s. Tens of millions will needlessly suffer or die. For what? Ideological drive lacking spiritual guidance? A lack of foresight? Oil?

Furthermore, are not the great powers, India, China, the USA, NATO, Turkey, Russia, and the EU building up military resources unseen since the second world war? Are these same powers now not hampering and shifting trade around the world, threatening the developing world especially with starvation and privation? If the mass media were not spreading *"news"* around the world, would anyone even know? At this point the only thing holding us back from this brink is whether the media chooses to convince us to accept this war as necessary and inevitable. It will all be lies.

We seem to be between 1901 and 1914, though the scales are twisted, stretched and compacted in various manners which make discernment difficult. The Queen is dead. Long live the King. The Great powers gather for a great dance of swords. We in the west (though we are hardly unique in being this way) have incompetent, out of control leadership, willing to flout the rights guarantees laid out in our founding documents, having zero qualms with resorting to extortion or violence as necessary means to ends. Canada is led by a middle-school drama teacher. The Great USA is led by a man suffering from dementia or Alzheimer's disease. The UK is led by a banking cartel lackey; while the EU is run by an endless parade of faceless bureaucrats. Like never before (or perhaps somewhat in line with the early 20th century) the *Western* state acts more like a mafia than a proper nation.

Discussion is done in secret. Opinions are actively withheld over fear of reprisal. Men and Women alike follow orders regardless of content to ensure their finances are unaffected. No real checks and balances are performed. The Judiciary defers to the mafioso state, despite its unfair material advantage. As a result, people begin to take extrajudicial action as their rights are not reasonably protected. Law becomes a tool of State policy rather than a set of abided principles used to guide action. Alternative forms of resolution become more and more popular as the legal system becomes less and less relevant. Eventually lawlessness becomes the de facto within the façade of the de jure.

Veni, Vidi, Vici

In such a scenario, a rising Caesar becomes less of a necessity and more of an inevitability, to return to a proper order of things, to some semblance of governance. In his will to action, he exercises exceptional powers to sweep aside the corruption and bureaucratic rot which has infected the power structure. Letting it be means to leave it to spiral, where it cannot self-correct. The inevitability of Caesar is obvious, and the only alternative is civilizational collapse. Whether or not a rising Caesar is legal in his actions, his actions are morally and ethically correct and necessary. The present interregnum offers nothing but decline. It offers no hope outside its shadowy façades. It threatens and damages peaceful, productive, and good people, while promoting the immoral and unethical, who are a social and civilizational danger. This is by no means anarchy, and is instead a kleptocracy veiled in unjustified authority.

If the alleged *"good"* people were to withdraw de facto support of the pretender-regime, it would eventually fail to stand. But a catalyst is required as it is in any reaction equation. Without this, doom awaits. It is therefore for the sake of civilization, imperative that a Caesar is brought forth. We must clear a path so should a man of the necessary calibre arrive, he finds the pathway to his destiny. Whether or not we succeed will depend on how persuasive our authoring is, and in turn this will rely on our capacity to accept or deny pain in reality. If you don't believe me, there is no need, nor am I concerned; *pain* will make you a *believer*.

CHAPTER TWENTY-ONE:

Cringe and Propaganda: The Bug Man Factory

The mass of natural man is a quivering batch of wild beasts bent on personal gain. Through history, the organizing principles found in religion brought this mass under control. The purpose of this control was not to domesticate man, nor weaken him, but free and strengthen him, thereby empowering him for the greater good. It was not the purpose to hammer man's swords into ploughshares, but to steel him against entropic ruin. In this essay I will lay out and discuss how cringe and propaganda act in combination to murder man's spirit, and how zealotry can help us step over both.

Cringe is a powerful tool. It is the second-hand embarrassment one feels when they witness something either embarrassing or disgusting (disgust being a low level form of hatred). In many dictionaries it is defined like this:

"...to bend one's head and body in fear, apprehension, or in a servile manner."

Note the words *"bend," "fear," "apprehension," "servile."* These are words of passivity, of a domesticated animal anticipating another beating. It describes a man who is completely broken.

To cringe is to be weak. It is to be controlled and manipulated into specified paddocks. It is to truly embody this as your whole being. It is the death of man, a return to the Edenic bestial unconscious form, guided there not by will or God, but by submission to evil, the fallen angels driving the beast-man into his cage to consume his *"feed,"* bread being a mere euphemism.

In this state, man is further weakened though this control over his fate, and eventually finds himself neutered, bereft of life force, rendered harmless to his masters; he has become the Bug Man. The Bug Man is no more man than livestock. His individual will has been subsumed through emotion and fear of loss and pain. He no longer consumes, but is fed. He is no longer willful, but driven by a neutered emotional impulse which he rationalizes post-hoc specifically to maintain a semblance of outward self-respect (though this is never internalized, as he despises himself); a task to which he also takes to drugs to numb the ever-present existential dread which seats itself upon the throne of his mind, clouded in the fog of vice to shield him from this realization. It is to live one's entire life in Hell.

In short, propaganda is the use of information to control emotions. People are susceptible to this in nearly every case, even those who are specifically aware of it. Propaganda is not always a bad thing. In past societies it has been used for the legitimate defence of a people or place against forces which might seek to destroy them. It often has positive results within a religious frame and is useful for imbuing inexperienced youth with useful morals and values which aid as 'a priori' knowledge guiding their actions and lives. But as man has fallen away from religion, much of this 'education' has been taken on by the State. This is a problem for a number of reasons. First, how does the State determine right from wrong? Currently all State laws are based upon a religious frame, but this has been collapsing as the managerial bureaucracy and politicians move to rationalize laws by another measure: "Science".

In effect what this does is not moral at all but instead attempts to re-state what values are, by a means which has none. Science is not in and of itself a system of moral judgement but one of material measurement. In the end the fall of religious bases of influence do not render a system which is more fair but one which is a monopoly in favour of the State. This means that by whichever means the State uses to rationalize into law or out of law, is no longer based on moral principle but unapologetic power. It makes "morality" not about law or fairness but about convenience and force.

Propaganda used to be checked through the competing power centres of Faith and State, but now the State is absorbing or has already absorbed the functions Faith formerly administered. Faith used to control and impose its will on the people, employing its tool kit upon the secular masses at its will. It is easy enough to see this happening in the West, but perhaps a contrast might help. Imagine the President of Iran decided to legalize "Gay Marriage" with all the power of the Head of State. Would it succeed? No! The Ayatollah would move immediately to remove him from power and likely with broad popular support, because in Iran the State does not have a monopoly on power. Compare that to the West, where we have marginalized our faith institutions. Could the Faith halt such moves by our own State? No. In fact most religious institutions have been totally captured by State power. "Religious rights" now exist only in as much as the State permits, and no more. To put it more bluntly, there are no religious rights remaining in the West. I suggest that this is the cause of our Civilizational decline.

Zeal is defined as a strong passion or faith in a cause; in short, *fanaticism*. There is no weakness in zeal, only strength. Zeal takes the strength of man's spirit and convictions and violently opposes meaninglessness and nihilism. It blinds itself to the dark drudgery of rationality, and casts a spiritual radiance upon truth as the highest ordering principle. Truth becomes God (and vice versa), and to fight for truth at all costs is to smother darkness in light. Power cannot withstand it, like a Witch to water, Power bathed in the light of truth dissolves a great Satan into mortal, corporeal men.

The Zealot is the entity most feared by the State. The Zealot is guided by pure faith principle. Reason cannot sway him. No force of darkness can withstand him, he cannot be wooed by propaganda. He cannot be manipulated by any entity outside of his faith. He crusades despite death, and he moves despite danger. He strikes existential doom into his foes and they can do nothing but attempt to dispatch him. But then from beyond the grave his power rises as a martyr and becomes an even greater threat to Power. It matters not even the particular faith as long as the principle guides *being*. Pagan, Christian, Muslim, Jew, Hindu or Sikh, the only successful weapon against faith is faith. To triumph over the faithless is easy, a matter only of time. The Zealot is the vanguard against decline.

Matthew 10:34

"Do not think I have come to bring peace to the Earth. I have come not to bring peace, but a sword."

Postmodern man is bathed in a sea of propaganda. With this is attempted by the State, for the first time alone at the helm, to neuter its own people, to murder their spirit, to cast its own infants upon the rocks and dash out their essence. It is worse than they treat livestock, for even their deaths serve a purpose commensurate with human beings. The spiritual massacre underway in the West is done not out of spite, but rationalised necessity. It is not cringe to care about your society. It is not cringe to care about being. Cringe is containment, it is the state of mind of the Bug Men. None are free from this burden until they choose to be freed from cringe. To cringe is to be paddocked like livestock, readied for spiritual slaughter! I appeal to your ZEAL, to feel. It is not cringe! It is real! Steel your soul against the forces of evil that see you as no more than dehumanized meat! Yours is the flesh reborn! Be not cow-towed towards your doom! Let your zealotry out, as Thomas Aquinas said;

"If you bring forth what is within you,

  what you bring forth will save you.

If you do not bring forth what is within you,

  what you do not bring forth will destroy you."

Like a wet blanket to a fire, cringe and propaganda comes to snuff-out your zeal. If those come for you, show them your zeal and set them ablaze in your radiant spiritual might.

Printed in Great Britain
by Amazon